The Text of
Chaucer's Legend of Good Women

The Text of
Chaucer's Legend of Good Women

BY

ERNEST F. AMY

*Assistant Professor of English
in Ohio Wesleyan University*

HASKELL HOUSE

Publishers of Scholarly Books

NEW YORK

1965

published by

HASKELL HOUSE

Publishers of Scholarly Books

30 East 10th Street • New York, N. Y. 10003

Library of Congress Catalog Card Number: 65-21088

PRINTED IN UNITED STATES OF AMERICA

PREFACE

Though the justification of this textual study of the *Legend of Good Women* is its conclusion, the necessity for such a study becomes apparent from the following facts:

1. The two standard texts of the poem—Skeat's Oxford Chaucer [1] and Pollard's Globe Edition [2]—vary considerably. A preliminary comparison of about a third of the text of these editions revealed variations—major and minor—in about eight per cent of the lines. Skeat's text is confessedly eclectic; Skeat states that after collating six MSS. he discovered that the best way to construct a text was to consult first G and F, "and then to see how the other MSS. support them." [3] Pollard's text is supposedly a critical one, though the student is at a loss to know how much faith can be put in it; for Mr. Pollard not only does not publish a genealogical tree, but he does not even state what he assumes the relationship of the various groups of MSS. to be. A cursory examination of portions of his text shows that the basal MS.—F—wields great authority in settling disputed readings; but whether this authority is justified is left entirely to conjecture.

2. A slight acquaintance with the MSS. leads one to suspect the accuracy of the genealogical tree of Siegfried Kunz's doctoral dissertation, *Das Verhältnis der Handschriften von Chaucer's 'Legend of Good Women'* (1889); for it presupposes the existence of the two forms of the *Prologue* in at least two transcripts (not counting the original), and it can account for the absence of lines 960-1 from six MSS. only as due to independent omissions by two well defined groups. [4]

3. Mr. J. B. Bilderbeck's detailed study [5] of the MSS. is in the main an attempt to prove that G represents an early

[1] *The Works of Geoffrey Chaucer,* Vol. III (Clarendon Press, 1894).
[2] *The Works of Chaucer,* Globe Edition (Macmillan and Co., 1898).
[3] Oxford Chaucer, III, lv.
[4] FTB and CAS(Ad)—Ad begins at 1640. See Appendix for Kunz's genealogical tree.
[5] *Chaucer's Legend of Good Women,* London, 1902.

draft of the *Prologue* and of at least the first six legends. Unfortunately for Mr. Bilderbeck's conclusions, Mr. J. L. Lowes shortly afterward proved conclusively to most Chaucerian scholars that the version of the *Prologue* in G represents the *later,* rather than the earlier, form.[6] If such be the case, one may justly suspect that Mr. Bilderbeck was likewise mistaken regarding the revision of the six legends; for he found that "the differences between the readings of G, and of the other authorities in the case of the legends are, in many instances, of the same nature as the differences in the readings of the two Prologues."[7] One is led to wonder whether his notion that G represents a primitive text has not colored his whole work to such an extent that his conclusions concerning the relationship of the MSS. and his suggestions for establishing a critical text may not also be untrustworthy. His work is still further unsatisfactory in that he refuses to draw a genealogical tree, because of evidence that the texts of certain MSS. are of a composite character.[8]

Because of the untrustworthy and unsatisfactory nature of Mr. Bilderbeck's and Mr. Kunz's work and of the Skeat and Globe editions of the poem, it appeared desirable to make an independent study of the MSS. and their interrelations and—if the results of that study warranted it—to construct a critical text. This dissertation is the record of that study. It is based upon a complete collation of all the MSS. as printed in the Chaucer Society Publications and a subsequent examination of the MSS. themselves. I have verified from the MSS. all the important readings upon which my arguments are based. (The Chaucer Society prints are in general to be trusted; I have listed the most important errors in an appendix to this dissertation.)

The validity of the conclusions of such a work as this depends upon accuracy of classifying and transcribing details, and judgment. Unwilling to trust my own judgment exclusively, I have frequently sought the advice of my friend, Dr. Henning Larsen, to whom I am indebted for many valuable suggestions. To Professor Thomas Marc Parrott, who read the dissertation in manuscript, I am under obligation for much

[6] See *P.M.L.A.,* XIX, 593ff.: XX, 749ff.

[7] Bilderbeck, *op. cit.,* p. 36.

[8] See Appendix for a discussion of Bilderbeck's work.

helpful criticism and advice.   But I am under greatest obligation to Professor Robert Kilburn Root, who guided my work
from its beginning, helped me solve many of the knotty
problems, and generously assisted in the uninspiring task of
verifying my transcriptions from the prints of the MSS.

Delaware, Ohio, May, 1917.

ERNEST F. AMY.

LIST OF ABBREVIATIONS

Manuscripts and Editions.

A: Additional MS. 9832, British Museum (1-1985).
Ad: Additional MS. 12524, British Museum (1640-end).
B: Bodley MS. 638, Bodleian.
C: Trinity College, Cambridge, MS. R. 3. 19.
F: Fairfax MS. 16, Bodleian.
f: Cambridge University Library, MS. Ff. 1. 6 (*Thisbe*, 706-923).
G: Cambridge University Library, MS. Gg. 4. 27.
M: Additional MS. 28617, British Musuem (513-610; 808-1105;
     fragments of 1156-1173, 1180-1192, and 1271-1280; 1306-1801;
     1852-2113; 2125-2136; 2151-end).
P: Pepys MS. 2006, Magdalen College, Cambridge (1-1377).
R: Rawlinson MS. C. 86, Bodleian (*Dido*, 924-1367).
S: MS. Arch. Selden, B. 24, Bodleian.
T: Tanner MS. 346, Bodleian.

Y, Y_1, Y_2: See diagram on p. 49.
Z: See diagram on p. 49.

Gl: Globe Edition, 1898 (Macmillan and Co.).
Sk: Skeat's Oxford Chaucer, Vol. III (Clarendon Press, 1894).
Th: Thynne's Edition, 1532 (Reprinted in the Chaucer Society
     Publications, First Series, LVIII).

Poems of Chaucer. (References are to lines in Skeat's Oxford
    Chaucer).
C. T.: The Canterbury Tales.
Comp to L.: A Compleint to his Lady.
L. G. W.: The Legend of Good Women.
M. B.: Merciles Beautè.
P. F.: The Parlement of Foules.
R. R.: The Romaunt of the Rose.
T. C.: Troilus and Criseyde.

    When letters are printed solid—as CASAd—a common ancestor
of the MSS. is signified; when commas separate the letters—as C,A,F,
M,G—the MSS. are referred to as individuals.
    Parentheses enclosing an abbreviation for a MS.—as FT(B)—
indicate that the MS. in question agrees with the others cited as
regards the word or phrase under discussion, but disagrees in some
other respect. Thus, "928. S, (R): Ouide *for* Eneyde" signifies that
S and R agree in the erroneous reading *Ouide,* but that R is also
corrupt in some other respect (R adds *Supporte*). I make an exception to this rule as regards spelling; I give the spelling of the

MS. first named and do not note the variant spellings unless they are significant.

In my tables of erroneous readings I give the corresponding correct readings as they are spelled by F, whenever possible. Thus, in the citation above, *Eneyde* is the spelling of F. When F itself is in error, as in the FTB and FB tables, I give the spelling of G. Exceptions to these rules are noted.

An asterisk (*) before the number of a line indicates an important instance.

The references to ten Brink's *Language and Metre of Chaucer* are to sections unless otherwise noted.

CONTENTS

THE TEXT OF CHAUCER'S LEGEND OF GOOD WOMEN

CHAPTER I

DESCRIPTION OF THE MANUSCRIPTS

G—MS. Gg. 4.27., University Library, Cambridge. Vellum, 516 leaves (plus 35 added later) 12 3/8 by 7 3/8 inches. The *Legend of Good Women* occupies leaves 445-480; it is printed in the Chaucer Society Publications, First Series, LVIII and LXI.

For contents of the MS. see Furnivall, *Temporary Preface* (Chaucer Soc. Publications), p. 7, or Miss Eleanor P. Hammond, *Chaucer: A Bibliographical Manual*, p. 189.

Furnivall dates the MS. at about 1430-40.[1] It is of especial interest as containing an important text of the *Canterbury Tales,* a unique version of the Prologue of the *Legend of Good Women,* and an appendix to Lydgate's *Temple of Glass,* known as the *Compleynt,* and found in only one other MS.

The value of the text of the *L. G. W.* has been variously estimated. Skeat states that it is "altogether the oldest, best, and most important of the existing copies of the Legend"[2]; Bilderbeck characterizes it as "without doubt the best authority for the lines which, as far as can be ascertained, do not appear to have undergone modification"[3]; but Koch says that it is "by no means a trustworthy MS., it has a good many acceptable readings indeed, but on the other hand it often enough spoils the sense and metre entirely."[4]

The G Prologue is 34 lines shorter than that of the other MSS.; for, while the G version contains many lines not found in the other versions, it omits even more. In the body of the poem G omits two couplets—1922-3 and 2506-7—which are found in the other MSS., and places the couplet 1738-9 after line 1743 (without seriously upsetting the sense of the passage). Leaf 469 is missing, involving the loss of lines 1835-

[1] *Temporary Preface,* p. 51.
[2] Skeat, Oxford Chaucer, III. xlviii.
[3] Bilderbeck, *Chaucer's Legend of Good Women,* p. 47.
[4] Koch, *Chronology* (Chaucer Soc. Pubs.), p. 82.

1907. This MS. possesses the couplet 960-1, which is found elsewhere only in P, R, and M.

Furnivall's conclusions concerning the dialectal and orthographical peculiarities of the G text of the *Canterbury Tales*[5] (which immediately precedes that of the *L. G. W.*) hold good for the G text of the *Legend* also. The scribe frequently substitutes *e* for short -accented *i*—*pete* for *pite* (491, 1080, 1097, 1324); *dede* for *dide* (1516). In inflectional endings the vowel is usually *i* or *y*, though occasionally *e* is used—*ensaumples* (1258). The guttural continuant is represented by ʒ, *myʒte* (935), *h*, *bryhte* (163), *gh*, *sleyghte* (931), or is omitted altogether, *sleyte* (1650). The character þ is rarely used. *Sch* is commonly written for *sh* in the first half of the poem.[6]

Of more importance than the dialectal and orthographical peculiarities are the peculiarities of the scribe as a workman. A glance at the early pages of the Chaucer Society print of the MS. reveals a relatively large number of textual changes. Unfortunately, Furnivall does not indicate the changes which occur after line 923; but an examination of the MS. shows that the first third of the text is fairly representative of the whole. Most of these corrections are of a minor nature, concerning merely a single letter or group of letters in a word. But in some cases words or phrases have been corrected; and in one instance a couplet is affected (288-9). Occasionally the editor states that the correction is "in a later hand." But in the vast majority of cases we are left in doubt as to whether the correction was made by the scribe or by some other person.[7]

The number of these corrections which might possibly have been for metre or grammar is exceedingly small in proportion to the length of the poem. Consequently, we must acccpt

---

[5] *Temporary Preface* (Chaucer Soc. Publs.), pp. 51ff. Of the *C.T.* Furnivall says (p. 59), "as to the dialectal peculiarities of the MS., most are Midland, some Northern, * * * and they point to a place on or near the border of the two provinces as the district of the writing of the MS."

[6] Strangely enough, after line 1832 *sch* is very rarely used; I have noted but a single case—2328.

[7] In this connection it is worth noting a statement by Furnivall in *Macmillan's Magazine*, 27:390 (1872-3). He speaks of the codex of G as "largely corrected by a contemporary reviewer."

the unusual metrical and grammatical accuracy as characteristic of the scribe's transcription and of his exemplar. But
that this accuracy may be the result of an "editing" of the
text by the scribe is a possibility which must always be kept
in mind. Miss Hammond says of the G text of *P. F.*[8] that
"the scribe of Gg worked consciously, and in some cases successfully toward the betterment of the text before him."[9]

Whether the scribe worked consciously or not, his text of
the *Legend* contains some very unusual blunders. In lines
1936 and 1964, *e.g.*, G reads *Thesius* where *Minos* is very
evidently required. But, curiously enough, the normal metre
requires the trisyllabic word; if the obviously correct reading
is substituted, the lines are awkward, though defensible. It
is interesting to note that at about the same point, 1966, all
of the MSS. except two[10] (which clearly emend) read *Of
Athenys*, although the context demands some locality in Crete.

At times the Latin sources of the legends help us to determine whether a unique reading in G is correct or not. In
1339, *e.g.*, the G reading is perfectly possible; but an examination of the source[11] of the passage leaves little doubt that
the reading of the other MSS. is the correct one. In another
case—line 890—G and f alone present a reading which the
source[12] indicates is correct.

> (890) G: myn woful hande
> (f my *for* myn; *Rest* thy *for* myn)

But G secured *myn* through a correction[13] by a contemporary
hand; *i.e.*, the line has been "edited."

In view of the above statements it is evident that G must
be treated with both respect and caution. Inasmuch as it
presents a unique version of the *Prologue* and many unique
possible readings, and a text for the most part metrically and
grammatically accurate, it commands attention. But, on the

---

[8] Decennial Publications, University of Chicago, *On the text of
Chaucer's Parlement of Foules, VII.*, p. 23.

[9] I shall discuss this point later. (See pp. 50-1).

[10] C and A read "In mochell myrthe." Skeat adopts this reading.

[11] Virgil, *Aen.*, iv, 652: "meque his exsoluite curis."

[12] Ovid, *Met.*, iv, 148-9. "Est et mihi fortis in unum Hoc manus:"
It is possible that the mistake is Chaucer's. See p. 60.

[13] After examining the MS., I believe that G originally read *thy*.

other hand, its very uniqueness and accuracy involve it in suspicion. Just how far this suspicion is justified can be determined better after the relation of G to the other MSS. has been studied.

F—Fairfax MS. 16, Bodleian Library, Oxford. Vellum, 336 leaves 9 1/8 by 6 5/8 inches, in eights. "Written almost entirely in one hand," says Miss Hammond,[14] "a clear, firm professional script of the first half of the fifteenth century; the date 1450 is on the flyleaf in a hand apparently contemporary." Printed in the Chaucer Society Publications, First Series, LVIII.

For a list of the 39 entries see Miss Hammond's *Manual*, pp. 334 ff.

The MS. omits parts of lines 244-5, lines 249, 487, 846, 960-1, 1490, 1643, 1693, 1998, 2150^b-2153^a, 2193, 2338 (a spurious line takes its place as 2339), and 2475. It reverses the order of lines 211, 212 (perhaps intentionally), and places the third strophe of the *balade* after line 277.

The scribe appears to have been a careful and intelligent workman; for in almost every case in which a missing line was due to a similar error in the immediate ancestor of F, the scribe noticed the absence of the rime-word and left a gap to be filled in later. (The gap is always left—usually incorrectly—for the second part of the couplet).

For the most part the spelling of F is exceptionally good. For this reason the MS. has been the favorite basal manuscript of editors. Its chief orthographic peculiarities are a frequent use of *y* for *i*—*hyt, ys,* etc.—the loss, or the incorrect addition, of final -*e,* and the excessive use of double vowels.

Most of the errors of the MS. are inherited. Many of these are perfectly good readings, and can be detected as erroneous only through a knowledge of the relation of F to the other MSS. Unfortunately, a large number of these errors have crept into our standard texts, because of the preference given to F as the basal MS. To cite a single example: Sk. and Gl., following F, accept as the reading of 2583

[14] Miss Eleanor P. Hammond, *Chaucer: A Bibliographical Manual,* p. 333.

"And to this woman hit accordeth weel,"

rejecting a reading which fits the context better and which, as I shall show later, is better authenticated by the MSS.—

"As to these women it acordyth wel."

Neither editor mentions the variant reading.

B—Bodley MS. 638, Bodleian Library, Oxford. Paper with vellum covers, 219 leaves about 8 by 5 3/8 inches, in eights. "Written loosely, coarsely, unevenly, and in a very untidy manner * * * in more than one hand, or by the same hand at different times," says Miss Hammond.[15] Schick dates it about 1470-80.[16] Printed in the Chaucer Society Publications, First Series, LIX.

All of its 17 entries except the last are to be found in F, and in almost the same relative positions.[17] The significance of this similarity is explained the moment one notes the gaps in B. For, like F, B omits lines 249, 487, 846, 960-1, 1490, 1643, 1998, 2150^b-2153^a, 2193, 2338 (filled in with the same spurious line found in F), and 2475. Morever, B too indicates most of these omissions by leaving blank lines where the omissions occur. In addition to the lines omitted in common with F, B omits also lines 157, 262, 1345, and 1866,[18] and inverts the order of 1776, 1777. The B text is further linked with that of F through a common—though somewhat different—disturbance of certain lines in the *balade*. (See pp. 21-2 for a discussion of this point.)

The above statements would indicate that B shares also the textual peculiarities of F; and such is the case. But the individual errors of the MS. are relatively small; and, consequently, B occasionally preserves the correct reading when F goes wrong. There are many corrections throughout the text in another hand. Numerous comments are scribbled upon the margins.

[15] *Manual,* p. 335.

[16] Edition of *Temple of Glass* (E. E. T. S.), p. xx.

[17] For list, see Miss Hammond's *Manual,* p. 338.

[18] Skeat is wrong in stating (Oxford Chaucer, li) that B omits line 623.

T—Tanner MS. 346, Bodleian Library, Oxford. Vellum, 132 leaves about 9 by 6 ½ inches. "In several hands of the fifteenth century, but with borders and initials apparently by one workman," according to Miss Hammond.[19] Printed in the Chaucer Society Publications, First Series, LVIII.

Twelve of the fourteen entries of T are to be found in both F and B.[20]

T omits, with F and B, lines 249, 487, 846, 960-1, 1490, 1643, 1998, 2150^b-2153^a, and 2338 (substituting the spurious line found in F and B). But, unlike the F and B scribes, the T scribe has ridden over all of these omissions, leaving no gaps to indicate that the text is not complete. T lacks also the half lines 1378^b and 1379^a, and reverses the order of lines 2494, 2495.

What has been said of the orthography and grammatical forms of F is true, in general, of T also. The errors and emendations of the text of T have been mostly inherited. But T is free from many errors which mar the texts of F and B.

C—MS. R. 3. 19, Trinity College, Cambridge. Paper, 255 leaves 10⅝ by 8 inches, of which the *L. G. W.* occupies leaves 114-150. Late fifteenth or early sixteenth century, neatly written. Printed in the Chaucer Society Publications, First Series, LVIII.

For contents see M. R. James, *The Western MSS. in the Library of Trinity College, Cambridge*, II, p. 69ff.

The scribe has omitted lines 233-4, 332-3, 489, 960-1, 1627, 2202-3, 2287-92, and 2569^b-70^a.[21] He has reversed the order of lines 1732, 1733; 2016, 2017. The illuminated letters at the beginning of the tales have never been put in.

This MS. belongs to a group which shows traces of having been edited. At times the scribe substitutes for a perfectly intelligible reading another which is practically synonymous; thus, in 1926 and 1941, *For ever and ay* takes the place of

[19] *Manual,* p. 337.
[20] For list of contents see *ibid.,* 337-8.
[21] The statements of Skeat and Bilderbeck that 2569 is omitted are misleading.

From yer to yer; in 2117, 2567, and 2635 *pryncipally* supplants *aldermost.* At times the scribe changes the text to present an intelligible reading; in lines 1902 and 1923, *e.g.,* all of the MSS. have more or less trouble in understanding the meaning of *Alcathoe* (the name of a city): C boldly emends the reading, which was probably unintelligible in the parent MS., to *All the cyte.*[22]

That these changes were deliberate there can be no doubt. Moreover, they are fairly representative of the text as a whole. Fortunately, the MS. belongs to a well defined group, and can usually be checked and corrected from other MSS. Such is not always the case within the last five hundred lines of the poem; for C here is strangely erratic.

To the comparatively late date of the MS. must be attributed occasional inaccuracies in the inflectional forms of the verb and the incorrect use of the final *-e.* But in many cases it is clear that these grammatical inaccuracies are inherited, inasmuch as they are to be found in other MSS. which are closely related. To cite a single example: I think that I have detected a tendency of the group of MSS. of which C forms a part to omit the negative particle from expressions such as *ne - - - noon, ne - - - nat,* etc. (In some of the other MSS. this particle often contracts with a verb immediately following, if contraction is possible—*e.g., nis, nam, nadde, nath,* etc.; perhaps a misunderstanding of this principle was the cause of the frequent omission of the particle by C and kindred MSS.). See lines 5, 188, 191, 192, 369, 670, etc.

A—Additional MS. 9832, British Museum. It is thus described in the *Catalogue of Additions:* "On paper, of the early part of the sixteenth century; interleaved with a printed copy of the same poem." The interleaved copy is Thynne's edition, 1532. The codex consists of 47 leaves 10¾ by 7½ inches. The MS. proper (exclusive of the title page and fly-leaf) occupies 30 leaves; the remaining leaves contain Thynne's text complete.

This MS. is a fragment, ending with line 1985. It agrees with C in omitting lines 233-4, 332-3, 960-1, and in inverting

[22] In the readings cited, A agrees with C.

1732-3; it stands alone in omitting lines 166, 351, portions of 629 and 630, 865-72, 1255, 1517 (in place of which 1516 is repeated), 1744-6, 1783, 1895, and 1945, and in inverting lines 766, 777, and 1566, 1567.

The MS. shares most of the orthographical and grammatical peculiarities of C (even to the frequent use of capital *A* when it stands initially in a word). On the other hand, it introduces not a few independent errors; note, *e.g.*, the large number of omissions which are peculiar to this MS.

Some of the readings of A appear to be successful emendations. Sometimes these emendations are to be found in C also, the most important being that of 1210—*thus lat I ryde;* note also the "editing" of C and A in lines 1902, 1923, 1926, and 1941 (pp. 6-7) and in some of the lines listed on pp. 24-25. But at times A presents the true reading when the MSS. with which it should agree are in error; see 1006 (p. 17), 1074 (p. 17), 1382 (p. 67), and 1686 (p. 18).

S—Arch. Selden MS. B. 24, Bodleian, Oxford. Paper, 228 leaves 10 1/4 by 6 5/8 inches, of which the *Legend of Good Women* occupies leaves 152ᵇ-191ᵇ. Apparently in one hand up to the middle of folio 209ᵇ. Dr. R. K. Root[23] has shown that the MS. was probably written between 1488, the year in which James IV came to the throne, and 1513, the year of the death of Henry, third Lord Sinclair—for whom the MS. was probably written. Printed in the Chaucer Society Publications, First Series, LVIII.

For a list of its 21 entries see Miss Hammond's *Bibliographical Manual*, pp. 342-3, and J. T. T. Brown, *The Authorship of the Kingis Quair*, pp. 70-77 (this MS. contains the unique copy of *The Kingis Quair*).

The orthography and dialect of this MS. are plainly Scottish. On almost every page can be found examples of *sch* for *sh*, *quh* for *wh* (as in *quho, quhat, quhwill*), and of *cht* for *ght* (as in *thocht, rycht, knycht*). The scribe frequently —but not consistently—writes *a* for *o*, as in *thrawe* (1286), *overblawe* (1287); *th* for *ght*, as in *strenth* (1405, 2326); and *eu* for *ou*, as in *yneugh* (1458), *dreugh* (1495).

[23] *MSS. of Chaucer's Troilus* (Chaucer Soc. Publs., First Series, XCVIII), p. 43. See *ibid.* for a detailed description of the MS.

The scribe has a fair ear for metre, but he apparently did not understand the value of final -*e*. As a consequence, perhaps no other one of our MSS. presents so many minor emendations. The conjunction *that* is frequently inserted when the sense allows it and the metre appears—to the Scotchman—to require it. (Examples of these minor emendations are to be found in lines 175, 205, 244, 245, 379, 432, etc.) The most important of these emendations is that of line 1538, where the scribe adds *almychti* to a line which is short in all the other MSS. except G (G has evidently emended).

It is evident that the value of the MS. in establishing a critical text is greatly lessened because of these well meaning emendations. This is true of the sense of the passage as well as of the metre; for it is a plausible hypothesis that a scribe who is interested enough in his work to desire to present a transcription which is correct metrically will try also to present a transcription which is intelligible. Consequently, one should not be surprised to find an occasional reading in S which suggests a very different relationship for the MS. than that demanded by the vast majority of readings.

Ad—Additional MS. 12524, British Museum. It is described in the "Catalogue of Additions to the MSS. in the British Museum" for the years 1841-5 as being a small quarto, vellum, of the end of the fourteenth century. To be more precise, the MS. consists of 28 folios, 7 3/4 by 5 3/4 inches, of which the *L.G.W.* occupies folios 1-17 (middle). *Sismonda* occupies the rest of the MS. The text is written in a fairly neat hand, though the pages are darkened and frequently stained with darker blots. The MS. is printed in the Chaucer Society Publications, First Series, LIX.

As to the date of the MS., Mr. J. P. Gilson, Keeper of the Department of MSS. of the British Museum, informed me that the MS. was certainly not earlier than 1450; that it was later, for instance, than the Thornton MS. (which contains *Alisaunder* and other Middle English poems).

This MS. is a fragment, beginning at line 1640. From this point to the end of the poem the text is complete, excepting for an injured page which has partially destroyed lines 2454-63.

The orthography of this MS. offers many interesting peculiarities. *W* frequently takes the place of *u* or *v,* as in
Owyde, wpon, wntreuth; quh is sometimes used for *wh,* as in
quhat; y for *i* is common, occurring even for the personal
pronoun *I;* certain consonants (chiefly *f* and *s*) are often
doubled, as, *e.g., sso, sse, wyff, yiff, fful, llady;* double vowels
(chiefly *oo*) are fairly common, as in *goo, ffroo, ssoo, hee; yh*
is used initially for *y,* as in *yhe, yhere.* These peculiarities
mark the MS. as Northern.

The transcript is a fairly good one. Occasionally there
can be detected a tendency to emend. Three of these emendations are worthy of notice—1772-3, 2543-4, and 2696-7—for
they are virtually free paraphrases of the original readings. I
quote the three couplets:

Ad: (1772). ffor mawgre hyr she shall be my lemañ
      (1773). ffor alday hap helpith the hardy. mañ

    Rest: For mawgree hir she shall my lemañ be
              Happe helpeth hardy mañ al-wey quod he

Ad: (2543) And thys she seyde hym also as I reide
      (2544) That he was lyke hys ffader as in thys

    Rest: But sothely of oo poynt yet may they rede
              That ye beñ lyke youre fader as in this

Ad: (2696) Then shall I. blede allace theñ shall I. Dye
      (2697) And nedys cost thys thing most be

    Rest: Thañ shal I blede allas and (me) be shende
              Or nedes coste thys thing mot have an ende

M—Additional MS. 28617, British Museum. Paper.
Originally a MS. of about 56 leaves (7 ½ by 10 ½), of which
36 and a few small scraps of others remain. Very unusual
and individual type of hand, probably belonging—according
to Mr. J. A. Herbert, Asst. Keeper of MSS., British Museum
—to the third quarter of the fifteenth century. Printed in the
Chaucer Society Publications, First Series, LX.

The missing leaves involve the loss of lines [24] 1-512, 611-807,

[24] In a few cases, some words or letters remain and indicate the
reading.

1106-1305, 1802-51, 2111-2124, and 2136-2150. The scribe has omitted lines 1516-17 and 2338 (in place of which is a spurious line found also in F, T, and B). He has reversed the order of lines 1306, 1307; 1652, 1653; 2104, 2105.

This unattractive and much injured MS. has been almost ignored by editors of the poem. Pollard does not even mention it in his brief introduction to the Globe text; and Skeat apparently forgot it when he prepared the text of his 1889 edition. Presumably, neither editor has made use of it. This is unfortunate; for in spite of its fragmentary character it proves to be of great value in establishing a critical text. Its position upon the stemma is such that time and again it becomes the arbiter of a disputed reading.

But the important position it holds upon the stemma is not its only claim to distinction; its value is enhanced by its reasonably accurate use of M. E. grammatical forms. The scribe sometimes errs in his use of final -e and of the inflectional forms of the verb; but, upon the whole, his work is such as to indicate either that he understood Chaucerian usage or that he was a careful copyist.

P—Pepys MS. 2006, Magdalen College, Cambridge. Paper, 391 pages 10 5/8 by 6 7/8 inches. (Page 392 and two unpaged leaves contain indexes). In six hands (not including a single leaf in the *L. G. W.* in still another hand) ; the *Legend* was written by the second hand. The MS. belongs probably to the latter part of the fifteenth century.[25] The text of the *L. G. W.* is printed in the Chaucer Society Publications, First Series, LIX.

For list of contents see Skeat, Oxford Chaucer, I, 55-6, or Miss E. P. Hammond, *M. L. N.* XIX, 197.

The P text of the *L. G. W.* ends with line 1377. The break occurs in the middle of a page, which indicates either that the P ancestor was imperfect or that the P scribe tired of his work.

At the beginning of the *Thisbe* legend one leaf is missing, involving the loss of lines 706-776. The lines of the next

[25] For a description of P see an article by Miss Eleanor P. Hammond in *M. L. N.,* XIX, pp. 196, 7.

leaf, 777-845, are in another hand. Though the orthography of these lines is different from that of the rest of the text, the readings and the errors are characteristic of the MS. as a whole.

P omits lines 232, 437, 623, and 1275. It inverts lines 159, 160; 163, 164; and 788, 789. It preserves the couplet 960-1, which occurs elsewhere only in G, M, and R. In place of lines 249 and 487 (omitted by F, T, and B) P has lines not found in any other MS. The significance of these spurious lines in P becomes apparent when one examines the P text of the *Temple of Glass;* for in the text of that poem (which immediately precedes the *L. G. W.* in P) P has three new lines in place of lines omitted by F, T, and B, and omits one other line in common with them.[26]

P is the most carelessly transcribed of all our MSS., with the possible exception of its near relative, R. Almost every page testifies to the scribe's unfamiliarity with Chaucerian metre and grammar. Frequently a line can be read only as a jogging four-stressed verse; then again a line or a couplet like the following occurs:

> But her of was betwyn hem so longe a sermonynge
> The wheche was to longe for to make þer-of rehersynge.
> (1184-5)

It is obvious that such a text has but little value either for collation or for establishing a critical text. Because of its frequent omission or insertion of short words which do not essentially change the meaning of a line, its common disregard for the inflectional forms of words, and its mutilation of the metre, the P agreements with various other MSS. in erroneous readings must not be taken too seriously. Such agreements are significant in the case of unusual readings; but in the case of minor errors, the agreement may very well be considered accidental.

R—Rawlinson MS., C. 86, Bodleian, Oxford. Paper, 189 leaves about 11 by 8 ½ inches. The 32 entries are "in various current hands, late and slovenly," says Miss Hammond.[27] It contains only the legend of *Dido* (924-1367) of our poem; a

---

[26] Schick, ed. *Temple of Glass* (E. E. T. S.), p. xx.
[27] *Manual,* p. 185.

marginal gloss states that the legend is the work of Lydgate. Printed in the Chaucer Society Publications, First Series, LX.

R lacks line 1067, and reverses the order of lines 1042, 1043; and 1118, 1119. It retains the couplet 960-1 (as do G, P and M).

Since R shares the eccentricities of P, the value of its readings is small. The only independent reading of R which editors have considered is that of line 1126; in this line R and P read *gyftes* for *gestes* of the other MSS.; but R alone presents an intelligible reading of the line.

f—MS. Ff. 1.6, University Library, Cambridge. Paper, 185 leaves (new foliation) about 8 ¾ by 6 inches, of which the *L. G. W.* occupies folios 64-67. "In many hands, all late fifteenth century, if not later," says Miss Hammond.[28] The *L. G. W.* is all in one hand. Printed in the Chaucer Society Publications, First Series, LX.

For a list of its 39 entries see Miss Hammond's *Manual,* pp. 344ff. The legend of *Thisbe* (706-923) alone is to be found in this MS. At its close, in another hand, appear the words "Nomen scriptoris Nicholaus plenus amoris."

The scribe has omitted lines 886 and 889; he has inverted the order of lines 884, 885.

This MS. is not of much value, partly because it contains so little of the poem, and partly because of its peculiar errors. The scribe evidently did not work intelligently; sometimes he appears to have been ignorant of the meaning of a word— *wre, e.g.,* becomes *owre;* at times he loses entirely the rhythm of the line (see 798-9): and frequently he presents a very peculiar spelling—*attur* for *hotter, weppet* for *wept, condyth* for *conduit.* The presence of such forms as *gyffe strynth* (892), *sche lyftud* (882), *fursty mowth* (878), etc., point to a Northern or Midland origin.

Th—Thynne's edition, 1532. Reprinted in Chaucer Society Publications, First Series, LVIII.

[28] *Manual,* p. 343.

Thynne's text is almost complete, lacking only the elusive couplet 960-1, and the couplet 1326-7, which is found in all the MSS. Moreover, the text includes both the genuine and the spurious forms of line 2338. It is probable that Thynne had more than one MS. at hand when making his text; this would account for the almost complete text and for agreements in error with MSS. of various types.

In the following discussion of the relationship of the MSS. I shall seldom mention Th. For, after all, this is but an edition and can be of value to us only if it presents a text— or occasional readings—representing some MS. now lost. In my collation I have noted all the variations of Th from one or more of the MSS., and I have come to the conclusion that its text can be constructed almost word for word from the texts of the existing MSS. The exceptions are almost negligible; the only ones of importance are the reading of *Alcathoe* (1902, 1923, which all of the MSS. stumble over,[29] and of *Chorus* (2422) for *Thorus,* or *Thora,* of the MSS.

[29] This statement is not quite true as regards G; for a leaf of its text has been lost where the first instance occurs, and the couplet 1922-3 has fallen out. The omission of this couplet, however, may indicate that G too stumbled over an unintelligible text; for only one other couplet is missing from the whole of the G text.

CHAPTER II

RELATIONSHIP OF THE MANUSCRIPTS

The foregoing study of the characteristics of the MSS. has brought out two facts of unusual significance, *viz.*, that G presents a unique version of the *Prologue,* and that all the MSS. except G,M,P, and R omit the couplet 960-1. It is obvious that we must attempt to interpret these facts before examining in detail the relationship of the MSS.

The origin of the two types of MSS.

The two forms of the *Prologue* suggest two types of MSS., which may have originated in one of three ways: (i) they may have descended from Chaucer's original MS. along independent lines; (ii) they may have descended from a MS., removed from Chaucer's original by one or more generations, which contained both forms of the *Prologue;* (iii) one of them may have been a composite.

We can accept the first of these theories only if we fail to find transcriptional errors common to both types, except such as can be explained as due to contamination, to coincidence, or to confusion in Chaucer's original MS. The second theory is hard to accept because it presupposes a greater amount of duplicated labor on the part of the medieval scribes than is in accord with human nature. To be sure, it may be urged that after Chaucer's death some of his friends would desire copies of the *Legend* with both forms of the *Prologue.* However, the theory cannot be accepted unless there are found transcriptional errors common to both types distributed generally throughout the nine legends and (probably) traces of contamination in the text of the *Prologue*—for if the two versions of the *Prologue* existed in a succession of transcripts, it is very likely that words, phrases, or even passages of one would creep into the other. In favor of the third theory one can urge that a poem of the nature of the *Legend of Good Women* offers abundant opportunity for the transcription and circulation of selected portions—individual legends, for instance, or the *Prologue* and a group of legends. The existence of two legends separately (*Dido* in R and *Thisbe* in f) proves that portions of the poem did circulate as separate units.[1] But one can accept the theory only if one should find the two types agreeing in error in some parts of the poem and not in others. The natural units of such a composite would be the *Prologue* and the nine legends as individual units, or the *Prologue* as one unit and the legends collectively as another.

It is obvious that none of these theories can be accepted or dismissed until the texts of all the MSS. have been examined in detail. But during this examination the theories must be kept constantly in mind.

The significance of the absence of the couplet 960-1 from all the MSS. except G,M,P, and R.

The absence of the couplet 960-1 from certain MSS. admits of two interpretations: it may have dropped out of some MS. in the process of transmission, or it may have been inserted, by Chaucer or some other person, after the first draft of the poem had been written. If the former be true, the MSS. lacking the couplet are related; if the latter, the MSS. containing the couplet are related. The passage reads as follows (Globe text):

>   (958) So longe he saylled in the salte see,
>   (959) Til in Lybye unneth arryved he,
>   (960) With schepis sevene and with no more navye,
>   (961) And glad was he to londe for to hye,
>   (962) So was he with the tempest al to-shake.
>   (963) And when that he the haven had y-take, etc.

I believe that the couplet was a part of the original text; for:

I. With the couplet missing, *So* in 962 is practically indefensible;[2] yet every MS. presents 962 unchanged;

II. The copyist could very easily have overlooked the couplet—mistaking *hye* (961) for *he* (959), which he had just written;

III. The source of the passage clearly indicates the authenticity of the passage. Lines 958-1155 of our poem are based

---

[1] But, as will be shown later, neither R nor f can be traced back to Chaucer's original independently of the lines of descent of the other MSS.

[2] *So* might conceivably refer to *unneth* of 959 if the couplet be spurious. But it is clear, I think, that the couplet is not spurious.

upon Book I of Vergil's *Aeneid*. Chaucer is freely para-
phrasing throughout this whole passage. Thus

> Huc *septem* Aeneas collectis *navibus omni*
> *Ex numero* subit; ac *magno telluris amore*
>
> (*Aen.* I. 170-1.)

becomes the basis of the couplet 960-1; *sale tabentes artus*
(*Aen.* I. 173) suggests 962, etc. Such details belong to Chaucer's working copy; it is inconceivable that he would have
inserted them into a later MS.

For these reasons I regard the absence of the couplet from
C,S,A,F,T, and B as positive proof that these six MSS. are
related. For though it is possible that two groups of MSS.
may have omitted the couplet independently, as Kunz assumes,
the mathematical probability is overwhelmingly against it.
However, before asking the reader to accept this proof as
conclusive, I wish to submit a number of other readings which
tend to support it.

*Other readings in which C,S,A,F,T, and B, and sometimes
M,P, and R, are linked in error.*

In the following instances I regard G as correct (in some
cases M, P, and R agree with G; in others they err with the
MSS. which lack the couplet):

641.   G: Among the ropis rennyth the scherynge hokys
F,T,B: and *for* rennyth; S: than; P: thenne; C: raf;
A: rafe;[3] (M: *text missing*)

Though it cannot be said that F,T,B,S,P,C,A are linked in
error, it is not improbable that their readings represent individual attempts to emend a common error. (For a full discussion of this line see p. 58.)

1006.   G,A: than is the bryghte sunne
M,P,R,F,T,B,C,S: *omit* is

The metre requires *is*.

1074. G,M,P,R,A: he semede for to be
F,T,B,C,S: him semede for to bee

(In this and the preceding instance I think that A has
emended correctly.)

1139. G,P,R: But natheles oure autour tellith vs
F,T,B: For to him yt was reported thus
C,A: Had gret desyre. And aftyr fell hit thus
S: And in his hert than he seid rycht thus
(M: *text missing*)

[3] The Chaucer Society print has *rase* (wrongly).

17

C,A and S evidently filled in an imperfect or an entirely blank line. Of the other two readings, that of G,P,R is the more Chaucerian. (See p. 99 for a full discussion of this line.)

    1269.   G: And waytyn hire at festis & at dauncis

                 C,A: And plesyn . . . (*Emendation from* 1265?)

      S,F,T,B,P,R: *omit verb* (M *lacking*)

    1330. G: Thus he hath laft dido in wo & peyne

The other MSS. read *And thus* (hypermetrical). To secure a metrical line, M omits *he* and C,S,A,P,R omit *hath.* F,T,B read *And thus hath he* (long).

    1391. G: As shal the goode man that therfore hath payed

The other MSS. omit *hath* and (except M) read *good* (M *goode*), which makes the line short. Though *the goode man* is a possible reading, I agree with Skeat (Oxford Chaucer, III. 325) that Chaucer has in mind here *good-man*, i. e., 'householder.' In that case G alone is metrical, except that it errs in reading *goode* for *good*.

    1405. G: Of fredom & of strenthe & lustynes

          F,T,B,C,S,A,M *om. first* & *and add* of *before* lustynes

G alone presents a metrical line.

    1449. G,S: folk that thow

          F,T,B,C,A,M *om.* that

Some of the MSS. read *folke*, which gives a metrical line; but the plural of *folk* is *folk* (ten Brink, 206). G also omits *And* at the beginning of the line—perhaps correctly.

    1686.   verry G: verry trewe

                S: worthy

         trew A: trew

        F,T,B,M,C: very

G alone is metrical. This would be a clear case in which G alone is correct, were it not for the reading of A. There are a few other lines in which A agrees with G against F,T,B,C, and S (see 1006 and 1074 above). The agreements are not so frequent as to suggest contamination.

    2408.   G: Ful of his folk

      Rest: Ful of folk

G presents a normal line; the rest, a headless one. *His* strengthens the sense as well as the metre.

    2482.   G: for on to philis ʒit ne come he nought

      S,Ad: For to phillis agayn ʒit com he nocht

      Rest: For vnto Phillis yet come he noght

S,Ad have emended for metre. I regard G as correct.

In addition to the above lines, in which G has the better readings, there exists a number of lines in which two readings are equally good. The most important of these are as follows:

794.   G,P,f: And so gret haste
             F,T,B,C,S,A: lykynge *for* haste

1107.   G: Of riche beddis & of ornementis
             F,T,B,P,R: . . . . . . of pavementʒ
             C,A (*emending?*) : . . . . . . other ornamentes
             (M *lacking*)

(See p. 40 for a discussion of these variants.)

1115.   G: for to iuste
             P: the Iuste
             R: the Iustis
             A: Iustynge
             F,T,B,C,S: the Iustyng

1178.   G: if that ʒe rede it me
         C,P: yef ye rede me
         Rest: yif that ye rede me

1187.   G,P,R,M: for no thing
         F,T,B,C,S,A: for no wyght

1217.   G: bestys wilde
         C,S,A,P,R: wilde bestys
             F,T,B: wilde hertes
             (M *lacking*)

1235.   G,P,R: and chaunge hire for no newe
         F,T,B,C,S,A: *om.* hire
             (M *lacking*)

1418.   G: To syndyn him
             C,A: To send him
               S: That for to send him
         M,F,T,B: That to senden him
         (P *breaks off at* 1377)

G alone has a perfectly metrical line.

1523.   G,S: euyl ymagynacyoun
             C: other ymaginacion
             M: other evyll ymagynacioun
         Rest: any other ymaginacion

Any other occurs in the preceding line. Since S and M have *euyl,* it is not unlikely that the other MSS. (or groups of MSS.) caught *other* or *any other* from the preceding line independently.

1525. G: That to the sunne he hath hym vp areysid

The other MSS. read *reysed,* thus lacking one syllable.

1701. G: No man dide there no more than his wif

The other MSS. omit the second *no* (M: *No man dydde more there*).

1821.   G: worthi
Rest: verray (werray)

2356.   G: She coude rede
Rest: She (*or* And) coude eke rede

The second of these lists could be extended. Examples enough have been given, however, to illustrate my point, *viz.*, that G frequently presents a reading as good as the readings of the other MSS. although it cannot be said to be correct. In some cases G may have emended for metre—in 1701 and 2408 (first list), *e. g.*, it may have patched up headless lines. But G presents so many headless lines (often when the line is regular in other MSS.) that I am inclined to believe that the G scribe recognized the headless line as Chaucerian.[4] (The significance of the occasional agreement of G with P,R,M, and f will become apparent later.)

Though some of the evidence submitted above may reasonably be looked upon as doubtful, most of it, I believe, must be accepted as corroborating my statement that the absence of the couplet (960-1) from F,T,B,C,S, and A is positive proof that those MSS. form a separate group. To these MSS. must be added Ad (which begins at 1640); for in all the readings between 1640-end cited above, Ad agrees with these six MSS. For convenience, I shall speak of this group as *Z*. Whether the occasional agreement of M,P, and R with *Z* signifies that they, too, stand apart from G can be determined better after the interrelationship of the MSS. of *Z* is known.

The relationship of F,T, and B.

Some of the erroneous readings cited in the foregoing tables suggest that F, T, and B form a definite sub-group of *Z*. This evidence is supported by the following:

I. The omission in common of lines 249, 487, 846, 1490, 1643, 1998, 2150^b-2153^a, and 2338;

II. The presence of a spurious line in place of 2339;

III. The agreement of the three MSS. in a large number of erroneous readings, of which the following are the most significant:

---

[4] See pp. 50-51 for a discussion of the headless line in G.

5*329. translatyd *omitted*
*(531. *the same Latin marginal note*)
  793. hath *om.*
*1085. in this manere *for* as ȝe may here
*1139. For to him yt was reported thus *for*
       But nathles oure autour tellith vs (*See p.* 99)
 1145. make *for* take
 1327. upon *for* unto
*1382. sleighte *for* sekte (T: seite)
 1386. and gretter *for* loue and
*1396. Ouyde *for* Guydo
 1397. knyght *for* kyng
 1512. the *inserted*
 1517. the   "
 1525. hyt *for* hym
*1730. on these *for* on the sege (G *corrupt*)
*1736. hevytee *for* (h)oneste (T: hevynesse)
*1747. bounte *for* shap
 1795. swerde *for* poynt
*1798. fayneth a love *for* fynt a lomb
*1881. the londe *for* that
 1949. contree *for* court
 1965. toward *om.*
*2008. asleked *for* achokid
 2019. that he *om.*
 2020. stede *for* drede
*2025. sarmoun *om.*
*2064. dede *for* deth
*2249. baste *for* lyst
 2286. longeth *for* lovith
*2297. ·dere *for* here
 2325. of hire *om.*
 2360. stames *for* stamyn
 2404. is *om.*
 2440. contree *for* court
*2491. Dispenden *for* Ne spende
*2615. of soun *om.*
*2619. ryght *om.*

The sub-group FTB can be further subdivided into T, and FB. As evidence I submit the following facts:

I. F and B omit lines 2193 and 2475, both of which are to be found in T;

II. F and B both bungle certain lines in the *balade;*[6]

---

[5] The asterisk indicates the clearest or most important cases.

[6] F,T, and B omit line 249 (in T the line is inserted upon the margin later). The rest of the text of T is perfectly normal. But the texts of F and B are very much disturbed. F has the third strophe of the *balade* after line 277, *i. e.,* in the body of the narrative. B not only

III. F and B agree in a number of erroneous readings which are either correct in T or, if incorrect, vary in another manner; the following are the most significant:

    1. men *omitted*
    40. such a *for* eke this (T *omits* this)
  *183. men by reson wel *for* well by reson men
  *314. sir *om.*
  364. But *om.*
  855. it *om.*
  *973. knytte *for* cutte
 *1063. and *for* hadde
 1258. ensamples olde *for* olde ensaumples (T *omits* olde)
 *1382. sleight *for* sekte (T—seite)
 1642. there *for* here
 *1681. dedes *for* doingis
 1685. and *om.*
 *1736. hevytee *for* (h)oneste (T—heuynesse)
 1987. that *inserted*
 *2291. bounde *for* beute
 *2328. longe *for* loude
 *2561. as in love truste *for* trustyth as in love (T—trusteth nowe in loue)

But T could not have been the ancestor of FB; for

I. T omits the half-lines 1378^b-1379^a, which are found in FB;

has portions of the *balade* within the body of the narrative, but it even fails to present the lines of the *balade* in their proper order. The order of the lines in F is as follows:

```
                  249 (omitted)
(1st strophe) 250-255 (correct)
(2nd    "   ) 256-262 (   "   )
(narrative  ) 270-277 (misplaced)
(3rd strophe) 263-269 (   "   )
                  278 ff.
```

In B the order is as follows:

```
                  249 (omitted)
(1st strophe) 250-255 (correct)
(narrative  ) 270-277 (misplaced)
(3rd strophe) 263-267 (   "   )
(2nd    "   ) 256-261 (   "   )
(2nd    "   ) 262 (omitted)
(3rd    "   ) 268-269 (misplaced)
                  278 ff.
```

The confusion is two-fold. F,T, and B all lack line 249; consequently that line must have been lacking from their common parent, FTB. The confusion in F and B is due, I think, to the fact that the FB scribe omitted the second and third strophes of the *balade,* and that later some one wrote them on the margin. But the position of 14 lines crowded on the margin is likely to be confusing. The F scribe put them into his text in one position; the B scribe chose another, missing 262.

II. T reverses the order of lines 2494, 2495, which FB presents correctly;

III. T has a few erroneous readings which are correct in the FB text; I submit the following (see also the T variations above):

*   97. þine *for* ӡeve
* 357. causes þey ben *for* ben the causes
* 378. harme *om.*
  807. and *for* of
*1063. routhe *om.*
*1181. lyfe ordeyne *for* leue or deye (F *spells thus*—lyve or deyn)
 1320. yif *for* ӡeue (F—yive)
*1389. tendere *om.*
*2188. hert *for* he(e)r

Some of the omissions and readings cited above indicate also that FB could not have been the ancestor of T. Consequently, the relationship of FB and T cannot be closer than that of sisters.

A further analysis of F and B reveals the following facts:

I. F alone omits line 1693 and reverses the order of lines 211, 212; B alone omits lines 157, 262, 1345, 1866, and reverses the order of lines 1776, 1777;

II. The F reading is sometimes wrong when the B reading is correct, as, *e. g.,* in lines *100, *792, 892, *1063, *1066, *1471; the contrary is frequently true, as in *373, 426, 744, *879, 1056, *1201, *1266.

For these reasons F could not have been derived from B, nor B from F.

The F,T,B relationship, then, is obviously this: F and B were derived from a common ancestor, which was derived from an ancestor of T.[7] The number of generations separating the three MSS. from their common ancestor cannot be determined; but the character and relatively small number of divergent readings, as well as the general agreement of the MSS. in grammar and orthography, point to an ancestor not very far removed.

The relationship of C,S,A, and Ad.

The other MSS. of group Z—C,S,A,Ad—are united by agreement in a few erroneous readings. Such, for example, are the following:

[7] The agreements of F and T, and of B and T in error are few and trivial; they can be accounted for as accidental. (See 777, 1313, 1776.)

380. as *for* and
388. bothe *om.*
448. I *inserted*
* 659. world *for* day
666. sweren falsly *for* falsely swere
* 741. there *for* deere
743. Thys *for* Ye (S—Thir)
744. They *for* Ye
907. Piramus of Tisbe *for* Piramus and Tesbe
1062. then *for* er
*1400. Eson *for* Pelleus
*1495. vs *inserted*
1607. art and craft *for* craft and art
8*1674. thought *for* youth (Ad *reads* youth)
*1739. worde *for* dede (S *reads* dede)
1803. holdeth (holde) *for* hath
1841. made *inserted*
2003. therto *for* also (S *reads* also)
2121. ye have *for* have ye
2441. dyd hym gret honour *for* dedyn hym honour (Ad *reads* hym they dede honoure)

The evidence for the subdivision of the group into C and A, S and Ad, is much more convincing. Thus C and A are connected by

I. The omission in common of lines 233-4 and 332-3;

II. The inversion of lines 1732, 1733;

III. The agreement in a large number of incorrect readings. I submit the following:

*88. herte *for* witte
*95. hertly *for* erthely
97. unto *for* yive
99. thyng *om.*
109. gret *for* glad
118. swete soft *for* softe swote
120. odour - - swetnes *for* suetnesse - - odour
130. byn *inserted*
188. wene ye nat *for* ne wene nat
230. hyr *for* his
*232. I saw a selcouth syght *for* his face shoon so bryght
*247. Then may *for* And therfore
303. coroun whyte *for* white corowne
*305. full of curtesy *for* ful curteysly
*348. and knew all *for* that knowen all

8 Ad begins at 1640. A ends at 1985. Evidence for connecting Ad to C,S, and A is not very strong. However, evidence for connecting Ad to S is so striking that one cannot doubt that Ad belongs to the group.

*376. But he that lord of kynges naturell *for*
      For he that kynge or lord ys naturel
 402. ryghtfull (A ryght foule) *for* ful foule
*480. to put the out of were *for* understond yt here
 493. hys seruantes charge *for* shal charge his servantez
 515. restoryd *for* rescowed
*525. I on *for* Ioue
*545. And hyt was preuyd in dede doing *for*
      And namely of wyfhode the lyvyng
*553. Ther shal no tru louer *for*
      Ne shal no trewe lover
 570. do al in *for* al yt
⁹*673. Of Rubyes And stones that best byn fyne *for*
      Of al the rubees and the stones fyne
*760. We kepe nomore *for* Yit woldestow
*765. throu thyn *om.*
*771. Orellys erly *for* Or wonder erly
 810. dredeful *for* drery
 811. drery *for* dredful
*830. And sodenly then in his hert hyt ran *for*
      And in his herte he sodeynly a-groos
*831. That erst was rody. pale he wexed And wan *for*
      And pale he wex therwith his heer a-roos
 834. bothe louers flee *for* lovers bothe slee
 853. Now thys Tisbe whyche *for* Now Tesbe which that
*905. And ryghtwys god graunt euery louer to sende *for*
      And ryght-wis god to every lover sende
*906. Trew loue more in gretter prosperite *for*
      That loveth trewely moore prosperite
*914. That of hys blood yet was all warme and hoot *for*
      That warm was of hire loves blood and hoote
 984. semeth *for* thynketh
*1053. that ys so meke *for* to beseke
*1089. Yow *for* Youre shippes
*1109. she had ete *for* he hadde seete
*1150. nobyll *added*
*1160. foote *for* theffecte
*1221. that they were agast *for* that ys so sore agaste
*1261. shame or gryef *for* some myscheefe
*1481. boot *for* cogge
*1690. The Austyn *for* The grete Austyne
*1697. dede *for* ydel
*1902, 1923. All the Cyte *for* Alcathoe
*1926, 1941. ffor euyr and ay *for* Fro yere to yere (A *omits* **ay**
      in 1941)

⁹ From this point to the end of the A text I shall quote but a few
examples of C,A agreements in error. Other examples are to be found
in lines 654, 656, 674, 676, 679, *684, *685, 695, *716, *735, *739, 752, 836,
843, *851, 858, *887, 970, 972, 976, *1107, *1139, 1249, *1252, 1253, *1258,
*1266, *1269, 1349, *1354, 1355, *1373, 1412, *1422, *1433, 1644, *1649,
*1663, *1664, *1667, *1743, 1759, *1764, *1770, *1774, *1786, *1790, 1810,
*1832, *1855, *1856, *1875, *1893, 1915, 1916, 1920.

Each of the two MSS. contains individual errors which prove that neither can be descended from the other. Thus, C omits lines 489 and 1627, which A retains; A omits lines 166, 351, parts of 629-30, 865-72, 1255, 1517, 1744-6, 1783, 1895, 1945, repeats 1516, and reverses the order of lines 766, 777; 1566, 1567;—all of which C presents correctly. Moreover, each text has a number of erroneous readings not found in the other. To mention a few examples: A is wrong, but C is right, in lines *190, 393, *565, *571, and *1085; C is wrong, though A is correct, in lines *252 (C and B[10] read *Marcia and Catoun* for *Marcia Catoun*), *1002, *1233 (C and R[10] om. *al his*), 1097, and *1672. It is evident that the relationship of C and A is no closer than that of sisters.

The two other MSS. of the group—S and Ad—are also related through ties of mutual error. No lines are omitted by the MSS. in common, but the following erroneous readings are to be found only in these two MSS.:

*1743. aroos *for* up roos; humble *for* blysful (CA blytheful)
*1871. every hie day *for* ever hir day
2012. ycrynklid is *for* is krynkeled
*2132. after *for* enforthe
2133. thair *for* his (thair caught from 2132)
*2163. salt see *for* wilde see
2174. stall away *for* stale hys way
*2253. at *for* al; wallis *for* balkis
2263. fast sche gan *for* gan she for
2299. þat is thy *for* and thy
2328. ful *om.*
2353. ywoued (Ad—woued) *for* wonid
*2367. And preyed hym by signes many one *for*
   And prayed hym by signes for to goon
*2368. Vnto the queene to go and bere that cloth *for*
   Unto the queene and beryn hir that cloth
2374. eke *om.*
2393. get *for* haue
2439. for the best *for* was the best
2477. In that month *for* in a Moneth
*2482. For to phillis agayn *for* For vnto Phillis
2483. hath *om.*
*2503. ȝede (Ad—yude) *for* went
*2523. cum *for* fal
*2526. false *for* faire
2531. to ȝow be (Ad—to be) *for* be to you

Since S omits lines 2226-7, which are retained by Ad, and

---

[10] These errors were probably made by the scribes of C and B, and C and R independently.

has a very large number of unique readings,[11] it cannot be the ancestor of Ad. Ad, on the other hand, reverses the order of the half-lines 2304^b, 2305^b, and presents several erroneous readings which have not found their way into S.[12] Consequently, S and Ad can have no closer relationship than that of MSS. having a common ancestor.

The evidence which I have submitted to show the relationship of C and A, and of S and Ad, indicates also the relationship of CA to SAd; for both CA and SAd contain errors not shared by the other and, consequently, neither can be the ancestor of the other. The closest possible relationship of C and A to S and Ad is that of cousins.

The genealogy of the MSS. of group Z may be represented graphically thus:

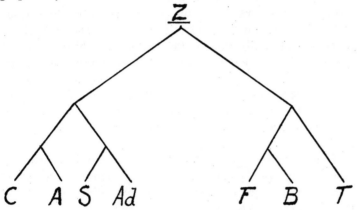

Exceptions to a classification of this nature are almost inevitable. But in this case the exceptions are for the most part unimportant. Only two need special consideration. The first of these is line 454, in which S and A read

God thank ʒow my lady here quod he;

the other MSS. read

Goo[Go] thank now my lady here quod he.

C should agree with S and A. Either C emended this line or S and A stumbled upon the same mistake independently (it is worth noting that the difference between *Goo* and *God* is not so very great).

---

[11] See 1887, 2010, 2011, 2091, 2140, 2317, 2340, 2392, 2481, 2499, 2626, 2720.

[12] See 1781, 1796, 1828, 1856, 1960, 2019, 2166, 2304-5, 2387, 2407, 2663, 2718; and see page 10 for comment on 1772-3, 2543-4, 2696-7.

In lines 85 and 108, S and A agree in minor errors which C avoids.

The other reading of importance occurs in line 928, where S and R agree in error.

> S: In thyne Ouide and Naso wole I take
> R: In thi Supporte ovide & naso will I take
> Other MSS.: In thyne Eneyde and Naso wol I take

I am inclined to think that this error arose through the similarity of capital O to capital E.[13] But whatever the reason, the agreement can be looked upon only as an interesting exception to the mass of evidence indicating that the two MSS. are not closely related.

The relationship of P, R, M, and f.
1. P and R.

Three of the four MSS. which preserve 960-1 are fragments. P presents lines 1-1377. R consists of *Dido* only, lines 924-1367, and thus runs parallel to the last third of the P fragment. But M has lost about 900 lines from the first third of the poem—1-512 from the *Prologue*, 611-705 from *Cleopatra*, 706-807 from *Thisbe*, and 1106-1305 from *Dido*.[14] Because of this fragmentary character of M, it is not easy to determine exactly the kinship of the four MSS. which contain lines 960-1.

Of the relationship of P and R there can be no doubt. Almost every fourth line contains an agreement in an error of more or less significance. I shall cite only a few of the most significant cases:

933. dede sterve (R—dide stryve) *for* must sterve
*939. brought to nought *for* fordoon and noughte (CA—to nought)
*943. and forth he ledde *for* and with him ledde
975. made *for* yformed
*978. quod she *om.*
*987. Or elles I trow thow art a goddes *for*
      And yf so be that thou be a goddesse
*1012. she was desyred *for* so desired
*1033. anon he gan to wepe *for* he brast out for to wepe
*1071. of flessh and bones *for* of brawnes and of bones
*1122. fair florence bete *for* floryns y-newe y-bette
*1126. (*a puzzling line*) gyftes; *Other MSS.* gestes
*1141. fadur (*of Cupid*) *for* moder
*1184. betwyn hem *inserted*

---

[13] See the facsimiles of late XIVth century writing reproduced in Thompson's *Greek and Latin Palaeography*, pp. 308-9, for examples.

[14] About 30 of the lines from *Dido* are only partially lost.

*1216. knyghtes *for* folke
*1220. and the light so fast *for* with haile and sleet so faste
 1224. sothly *for* shortly
 1256. fals *inserted*
 1258. so many *for* suche
*1264. wurthy *for* grete (S—ilke)
*1303. wull ye goo *for* wol ye soo
*1315. And (R—All) vnatired wyth her bright herre *for*
 Disshevely (Discheuele) with hire bryght gelte here
*1325. But al this pitows complaynt availleth ryght (R—*om.*) noght
 for
 But al this thing auayleth hire ryght nought
*1327. fro hir falsely *inserted*

But the disagreements between P and R are such that one
could not have been derived from the other. For example,
R is corrupt in

 1045. wrouth *for* brought
 1166. many a sighe *for* many a brayde (*rime-word*, sayde)
 1169. gan she say *for* spake she thanne (*rime-word*, Anne)
 1221. with hedowse fer *for* with heuenes fire

and many more, in which P is correct. Likewise P is incorrect in many cases[15]—including one omitted line (1275)—
in which R is correct. Consequently, P and R must have
been derived from the same corrupt ancestor.

2. *The influence of FTB upon PR.*

P and R, by virtue of their possession of the couplet 960-1,
should lie without the sphere of influence of *Z*. But such
is not the case; both MSS. show unmistakable signs of having
been influenced by an FTB ancestor. Note, for instance, the
P readings of lines 249 and 487, the only two lines of the
Prologue omitted by FTB. In the first instance the scribe
of P (or the scribe of a P ancestor) uses line 251 to fill the
gap caused by the absence of 249, and writes an entirely new
line to take the place of 251 ;[16] in the second case the scribe
inserts a spurious line of which only the rime-word is found
in the genuine reading.[17] There can be no doubt that these
two spurious lines represent gaps in a parent MS. And since
these lines are missing only from FTB, we have to assume
that for the *Prologue* P and FTB had a common ancestor.[18]

[15] See lines 968, 974, 1023, 1070, 1154, 1233, 1260, 1276, 1282, and 1312.
[16] 251 (for 249) P: Orpheus eke and Crudence thy feere. (*The
omitted line reads*—hyde absolone thy gylt tressis clere—*A spelling.*)
[17] 487. P: And how suche men full oft hem self assayen *for*
 That all here lyffe(ne) doth not but Assayne (*A spelling*).
[18] In the *Temple of Glass* P presents spurious readings in place of
three lines which FTB omit. (See Schick ed.—E.E.T.S.—p. xx.)

A closer examination of the FTB and P texts of the *Prologue* reveals a few agreements in erroneous readings. Though some of them may very well be accidental agreements, a few are striking. The list is as follows:

131. of *for* from
*196. thyng *for* strif (Thyng *caught from* 195?)[19]
212. I love so *for* I so love
345. be thus *for* thus ben
*371. And though *for* As thow
*404. dredful *for* sorweful
435. as *om.*
*436. never *for* no
457. the *om.*
*459. geue me *om.*

No further FTB influence occurs until near the end of the fragment. In the following instances PR agrees with FTB:

1269. F(T)B, PR: To hir at festes and at daunce(s); (T: And
      for To)
    G: And waytyn hire at festis and at dauncis
    CA: And plesyn hyr at festes and at daunces
    S: And hir at the festes and at daunces
    (M *lacking*)
1296. FTB, PR: me so sore
    G, S: so sore me
    A: sore me
    C: me so
    (M *lacking*)

(The text of M begins at 1305. M agrees with PR and FTB in the following instances.)

1319. so *om., thus giving a headless line instead of the normal
    line presented by G and* CS(A)—
    G, CS(A): And so ye wele me now to wive take
1339. now *om.*
1345. a *om.; it inserted*
1357. I make *for* make I
1363. Al be it *for* Al be it that (P: Al be that)
*1370. Ientil *for* tendere (R *ends at* 1367)

The P text comes to an end at 1377. We shall see soon that M continues to show an FTB influence until the end of the poem.

The two lists submitted above indicate that P was under the influence of an FTB MS. throughout the *Prologue,* and perhaps so during the last one hundred lines of its text. Between the *Prologue* and line 1269, there are no readings which

---

[19] If I am correct, this line cannot be used as an argument for the priority of the B version of the *Prologue.* Lowes should have noted that CSA, as well as G, reads *stryfe.* (See J. L. Lowes, *P.M.L.A.,* 19, 664-5.)

serve to connect P to FTB. A few lines suggest an influence from CSA, but they are not convincing. I submit them for what they are worth:

777. G,FT,f: Come Piramus and after come Thysbe
     CA,P: Aftyrward *for* after come
     S,B: after him *for* after come

784. CA: where theyr ⎤
     S: there-thaire ⎬ *for* here
     P: ther her ⎦

800. CA,P: Any woman *for* ever woman

808. CA,P,M: *om.* as

863. C,P: fast opon (P: on) the ground
     A: against the ground
     Rest: on (upon, unto) the ground

910. C(A)S,P,M: but yef (A: *om.* but)
     G,FTB,f: but

980. A,P: any other beste *for* or other beste
     R: and wyld best

1076. CA,PR: god doth bote *for* god do bote
      S: god wote

1147. G,FTB: is to here
      C: ys hit to here
      S: it is to here
      A,PR: it was to here

1215. CAS,PR: ones mete hym (*the better reading?*)
      G,FTB: hym onys mete

I am inclined to regard these agreements as accidental. They certainly are not striking enough to suggest a direct influence of some MS. from the CAS group upon PR; and they are not important enough to lead one to suspect contamination. I think that P stands quite apart from the MSS. of *Z* from the end of the *Prologue* to about line 1250 (1269 shows the first definite influence of FTB).

3. PR and M.

We have yet to consider the relationship of PR to M. I have already cited[20] a few cases—1319, 1339, 1345, 1363, and *1370—in which PR agrees with M as well as with FTB in probable errors. Earlier in the text of *Dido* I have noted a few more cases in which PR and M are wrong; they are as follows:

*925. M,PR: Bere thy name *for* Be to thy name

927. M,PR: How Eneas was to Dydo Forsworn *for* to Dido was
          for-sworne (A: was to Dido, *but om.* for-)

950. M,(PR): And to the see he gan hym full fast hye (PR *om.*
          full; P: cowde *for* gan; R: covde *for* gan)

984. M,PR: as thynkyth *for* as yt thynketh (C: as it semeth;
          A: as semeth)

20 See p. 30.

1020. M,PR: *om.* that
(M *lacks lines 1106-1305.*)

In the *Thisbe* fragment M presents a few errors in common with P (R does not contain this legend). I have noted the following (the M fragment begins at 808):

808. CA,P,M: *om.* as
[21]*810. G,FTB,S: Sche rist hire up with a full dredy (drery) herte
      CA: She arose hyr up with a full dredeful hert
      P: She rose in haste with a drery hert
      M: She roos with a drery herte
      f: Sche rose vp wyth a drewri hert
815. M,P: for *for* so (*Perhaps accidental*)
*821. M,P: wold she stynt *for* she ne stynt
824. M,P: at home allas *for* allas at home
910. C(A)S,P,M: but yef (A: *om.* but)
     G,f,FTB: but
     (*Either reading is possible.*)
*923. M,P: *add* love, *making the line hypermetrical*

The short fragments of the M text of the *Prologue* and of *Cleopatra* show no signs of having been influenced by a P-type MS. Nor do these fragments contain readings which would link them with any of our other MSS. In fact, except for the readings already cited, there is only one line in the M text of the first half of the poem which suggests an influence from a MS. belonging to the *Z* group—903, which reads thus:

903.   G: That in on grave that we motyn lye
   FTB,M: *om.* that (2)
   C(A): I-fere *for* that (2) (A: in fere)
   S,f: *om.* that (2); bothe *before* lye
   P: that we togeder lye

The source of this passage favors the idea of "together"—

O multum miseri, meus illiusque parentes,
ut quos certus amor, quos hora novissima junxit,
componi tumulo non invideatis eodem.

               Ovid, *Met.* iv. 155-7.

(Golding translates, "In one grave be together layd.")

It is evident that this line cannot be discussed profitably until the stemma is completed. For the present I need but say that I am not inclined to take the M,FTB,G agreement seriously, since it stands alone in this portion of the text (the strongest M,PR agreements follow almost immediately—923, 925, 927—and the couplet omitted by *Z* belongs to the same portion of the text).

[21] I regard the reading of M as the reading of an ancestor of M and P (and probably of f—the three MSS. om. *full*). P added *in haste* and f (perhaps) added *vp*.

32

4. *The influence of FTB upon M.*

After P breaks off, the M text is very plainly under the influence of an FTB MS. In addition to the six lines already cited[22]—1319, 1339, 1345, 1357, 1363, 1370—I submit the following:

[23] 1382. seeyte (FB: sleight) *for* sekte
  1418. That to senden *for* To syndyn (S: that for to send)
*1472. Where lay the ship *for* Where that the ship
  1524. *om.* so
*1649. *om.* ryth (ryght)
  1653. she ys goone *for* is she gon
*1668. neuere *for* ther
  1773. al way *for* alday
  1876. And in hire stable herte *for* And for the stable hert (G text lost)
  1971. compleynt *for* compleynynge
  2071. *om.* If
  2086. *om.* that
*2111. Forto taken *for* tacheue (to acheve)
  2186. gropith *for* graspith (Ad: gaspeth; S: grapid)
  2203. *om.* that
  2221. telle I *for* I telle
  2255. full *for* ek
*2338. ⎫
*2339. ⎬ *Inverted*
**2339. Huge ben thy sorwes and wondre smerte, *for*
    So that she myghte hym neueremore asterte
*2393. haue a nother *for* haue non othir
  2485. *om.* ryght
*2525. seyne *for* pleyne
*2592. And with *for* That what with
*2615. *om.* of soun
  2619. *om.* ryght
  2624. *om.* he
*2640. as seyne *for* as in
  2652. So hit be to me *for* So it to me be
  2684. streyneth hire so *for* hire streynyth so
  2721. *om.* hire

No one can question the influence of an FTB MS. upon M throughout the last half of the poem. The large number and distinctive character of these agreements make the absence of such from the first half of the poem all the more conspicuous. We must conclude that M is a composite, the dividing line occurring somewhere within the tale of *Dido*. Since M lacks lines 1106-1305 of *Dido*, it is impossible to state just where the FTB influence begins.

[22] See p. 30.
[23] Discussed on p. 67.

5. *Conclusions regarding the relationship of P, R, and M.*

To sum up the conclusions reached concerning the relations of P, R, and M. P and R are closely bound throughout the whole extent of the R text (*Dido* only). Their common ancestor (PR) appears to have been derived from an FTB MS. after (about) line 1250. The *Prologue* of P (or of its ancestor, PR) was also derived from an FTB MS. M contains a large number of readings which link it to FTB; but all of these occur after line 1306 (1106-1305 are lost); and those which occur between 1306 and 1377 (the last line of P) are also PR errors. Before 1306 there are a few errors in M which link it to PR; these are all in *Thisbe* and *Dido*. The short M fragments of the *Prologue* and of *Cleopatra* are noncommittal.

It is obvious that the simplest interpretation of these facts is that M and PR had a common ancestor which was a composite. One of the elements of this composite was an FTB-type of MS.; the other element was a MS. which stands apart from the Z group.

Judging from the text of M, MPR must have been an excellent transcript. But it came down to PR in a very corrupt form. R took *Dido* from PR and corrupted the text still more. P also magnified the corruption of PR, but tired of the work after 1377 lines had been transcribed.[24]

For the sake of convenience I shall speak of this composite MPR as "Y." The portion of Y which was derived from an FTB MS. I shall designate "Y_1"; the portion between the *Prologue* and line 1250 I shall speak of as "Y_2." I shall use the same subscripts to designate the corresponding portions of M, P, and R when I have occasion to speak of those MSS. separately.

---

[24] We have further evidence to support this hypothesis in the fact that the P texts of the *Hous of Fame* and the *Parlement of Foules* are also fragmentary; both are in the same hand (the second of six) as that of the *Legend*. Consequently, I think that it is more reasonable to suppose that the P text was fragmentary than the text of MPR.

It should be noted, in passing, that the head-pieces of the legends in M are in Latin and agree in the main with those of FTB. The head-pieces in P (there are only two) are in a later hand; they are in English and are connected with those of FTB through the word "martir."

6. The relationship of f to MPR.

The fragment f is almost non-committal as regards its relationship to the other MSS. I submit a list of all errors which may throw light upon the relationship of f:

738. f,G,T: cop *for* toppe (*probably accidental because "c" and "t" are nearly alike in most MSS.*)[25]

775. f,CAS: erbus swete[26] *for* erbis wete (*invited by the context*)

777. f,G,F,T: aftyr come (*correct?*)
    P₂,CA: aftyrward
    S,B: after him

*794. f,G,P₂: haste
    Z: lykyng (*See p. 39*)

796. P₂,f: *om.* full

798. P₂,f: All hyr frendes
    G: And alle hire frendis
    Z: For (S: ffro) al hire frendes

799. P₂,f: *om.* allas (P: *adds* grete)

801. CA,P₂,f: bettyr (*unimportant*)
    Rest: bet

803. P₂,f: that *for* this

*810. M₂,P₂,f: *om.* hire *and* full (M₂,P₂ *omit* up *also.* See p. 32)

815. M₂,P₂,f: for *for* so (P *otherwise corrupt*)

*855.   P₂: my love Pyramus ⎱ (*Was* myn owne *in an ancestor?*)
        f: my none pyramus ⎰
    G,Z,M₂: myn piramus

858. P₂,f: *add* she

859. P₂: *adds* also; S,f: *add* eke (*unimportant*)

864. G,S,f: therwith
    Rest: therwithal

[27]903. S,f: we motyn bothe lye (See p. 32)

916. G,M₂,f: is (f: his)
    Z: are (And thus are tesbe and Piramus agoo)
    P₂: *om.* are (*or* is)

As far as the evidence goes, P₂ and M₂ appear to be the closest relatives of f. (Unfortunately, lines 706-776 have been lost from P₂ and lines 706-807 from M₂, so that f can be compared with these two MSS. in less than 150 lines.)[28] The agreement of f with G and P₂ in 794 is important only if *haste* is wrong. The agreements of f with MSS. of group Z are purely accidental. One line (855) indicates that f is between Y₂ and P₂; but lines 821, 824, 923 (see p. 32.), and perhaps

---

[25] In f, however, the distinction between "t" and "c" is well marked.

[26] The *s* in *swete* is not the usual long *ſ* (used constantly when initial), but the medial or final *s*. It is bungled and blotted; I am not sure but that the scribe made a mistake and half cancelled it. The spacing between the words shows that it was not inserted.

[27] For the apparent agreement of f with G in 890 see p. 3.

[28] Though lines 777-845 of P₂ are in a different hand, they are from the same ancestor as the rest of the text.

810 appear to indicate that f stands between Y_2 and Chaucer's original. Since the matter is not of importance, I shall consider f as springing directly from Y_2. (See table on p. 49.)

The relationship of G, Y_2, and Z.
1. G and Y_2.

Before the position of G can be determined, two classes of readings must be examined—readings which appear to connect G with one or more of the other MSS., and readings which appear to be unsatisfactory in all MSS.

In the *Prologue* only one line calls for attention, 482. In this line both G and P_1 read *lyf* where the other MSS. read *tyme.* Since G possesses a unique version of the *Prologue*, and since one of the two strong links which bind P to FTB occurs only five lines later, the P reading must be regarded as due to contamination or coincidence.[29] In a few other cases (196, 261, 345, 404—see next chapter) CAS agrees with G where FTBP$_1$ has equally possible readings. Though it is not impossible that in these cases CAS has been contaminated from G, I am inclined to believe that the FTBP$_1$ readings are errors. Throughout the *Prologue*, at least, G is pretty definitely separated from the other MSS.

In the body of the poem the following lines must be considered:

794. G,Y_2: And so gret haste Piramus to se (P: for to see)
   Z: And so grete lykynge . . . (FB: Had *for* And)
  (M *lacking*)
831. G,P_2: his herte arose
  Z,M_2,f: his heer aroos (—CA)
  (CA *corrupt*)
1187. G,Y_2: Loue wil loue for no thing wele it wande
   Z: . . . for no wyght . . .

In addition to these, Bilderbeck suggests[30] a number of readings in which G agrees with P, as follows:

313. P_1,G: hym herd *for* it herde (hym *is invited by the context*)
449. P_1,G,SA: what *for* as
636. P_2,G: payned *for* paynen (M *lacking*)
671. P_2,G: wolde *for* wol (M *lacking*)

[29] Were there contamination from the G *Prologue* to any MS. having the unrevised *Prologue*, one would expect to find the contamination exhibiting itself in some of the major differences between the two versions. The agreement of G and P in 482 must be regarded as due to coincidence; such agreements in substitutions become significant only when the instances are numerous.

[30] Bilderbeck, *op. cit.* 68.

36

694. P_2,G,A: be well seen *for* wel be seene (M *lacking*)

871. P_2,G: tournement *for* tormente (M *and* f *exist*)

874. P_2,G: med(e)led *for* medeleth (M *and* f *exist*)

882. P_2,G,A: he *for* she (M *and* f *exist*)

(But in G "sc" has been "scratcht out," says Furnivall. In A, too,—though Furnivall does not note it—ʃ has been erased before *he*.)

960-1. Retained by G,M,R, and P (*i. e.*, G,Y_2). Bilderbeck thinks that Chaucer desired to cancel these lines. I regard the omission as an error of the Z scribe. (See pp. 16-17.)

1074. G,Y_2,A: he semed *for* him semed
    (*him* is certainly wrong)

1119. P_2,T: shined
         G: shynede (*alone metrical*)
     R_2,FB,SC: shyneth
         A: shone
    (M *lacking*)

1135. G,Y_2: presentis *for* presentynge (M *lacking*)

1139. G,Y_2: But natheles oure autour tellith us (P: thus)
     FTB: For to him it was reportyd thus
      CA: Had gret desyre. And aftyr fell hit thus
       S: And in his hert than he seid rycht thus

The reading of G,Y_2 is certainly more Chaucerian than the variants (see the parallel readings I have cited on p. 99). Bilderbeck suggests that Chaucer cancelled the line without indicating a substitute. It is more reasonable to suppose that the line dropped out at Z, and that the gap was filled in differently by FTB, S, and CA.

1235. G,Y_2: chaunge hir *for* chaunge (M *lacking*)
Either reading satisfies the metre and sense. There is no reason why the omission of *hir* cannot be regarded as an error of Z.

Bilderbeck says,[31] "It may be said that these readings are the results of accident, but the resemblances are too numerous to justify such a hypothesis." Let us see.

Bilderbeck is arguing that P is a hybrid, to which a MS. of the type of G contributed. We have already seen that P is most closely related to R,M, and f,[32] and that the ancestor of these four MSS. was a hybrid to which an FTB MS. contributed. It is difficult to explain the agreement of these MSS. on any other basis. Consequently, any agreement of P with G which is not supported by R, M, and f may well be regarded as accidental, unless it is of a striking nature. Keeping that in mind, let us examine Bilderbeck's list.

[31] Bilderbeck, *op. cit.*, 68.

[32] If f did not descend from the hybrid ancestor Y, it came from the ancestor of Y_2; my conclusions are therefore valid in either case.

Two of the readings are from the *Prologue*. The first agreement (313) is trivial and certainly accidental—the context invites *hym*. In the other line, 449, the testimony of *Z* is divided thus:

(449.) FTB,C: dooth wyth hym as yow liste
S,A: what *for* as (*So* G *and* P₁)

In either case two of the *Z* MSS. erred independently. The more natural mistake would be a change from *what* to *as,* for *as yow leste (as hym leste, as hem leste)* is a common Chaucerian phrase; the scribe would have used it twice within the 300 lines preceding this line; and it occurs several times in the remainder of the poem—615, 1244, 1703, 2042, and 2169.[33] *What yow leste* is less common, but not un-Chaucerian; it occurs in this same sense—but in a somewhat modified form— in lines 1113 and 2469. So upon the principle of *durior lectio* I should consider *what* as the reading of *Z* as well as of G and P₁.

From the other readings cited by Bilderbeck we must eliminate 960-1 and 1139 as certainly being from the original text, and 1074 and 1235 as probably correct. No argument can be based upon 882, for G and A have been corrected. In six lines—636, 671, 694, 871, 874, and 1119—the agreement of P and G is that of grammatical forms, word order, or spelling; in two of these cases, 871 and 874, M and f contradict P; in another—utterly trivial—1119, G may have the correct reading, though R fails to support P; and in the other three—all trivial—M,R, and f do not exist. In the list which Bilderbeck submits there is only one clear case of P agreeing with G in error, 1135, in which G, and PR read *presentis* for *presentynge*. I account for it as due to a natural error of writing the more common substantive for the verbal noun, i. e., p̄sēt͞yͦg became *presentys*.

The only other readings which indicate a connection of G with P are the three I cited first—794, 831, and 1187. In 831 *herte* is probably wrong;[34] but it cannot be regarded as the reading of *Y₂*, for both M₂ and f read *heere*. With *herte* occurring in the preceding line, the tendency to err is very

---

[33] All of these readings are well authenticated.

[34] *His herte aros* is not impossible. But I regard *heere* as being more probably correct because (a) it supplements better the first part of the line—*And pale he waxed;* and (b) *his herte aros* is almost a repetition of the thought of the preceding line.

strong. It is more probable that G and P_2 erred independently than that M_2 and f should have emended successfully.

The correct reading in the other lines, 794 and 1187, cannot be determined. Both *thyng* and *wyght* are colorless words; the probability of a scribe's substituting either one for the other is about equal. Between *haste* and *lykynge* there is also but little to choose. The source does not furnish any aid; nor does the context, unless the idea of impatience expressed in 791-2—

> And longe hem thoghte that the sonne laste,
> That it nere goon under the see adoun—

gives a clew to the working of the poet's mind. As regards 794 and 1187 I think that the question resolves itself to this: shall we accept the testimony of Z, which is frequently found to be in error, or of G, Y_2, which do not elsewhere (except for a few possible G, P_2 errors which cannot be laid at the door of Y_2) agree in erroneous readings? Upon the basis of such a test the probability is overwhelmingly in favor of the G, Y_2 readings being correct. And thus I regard them.

I conclude from the study of the readings which Bilderbeck submitted as evidence of a connection of G with P, that G is entirely independent of the MSS. of Y_2. I know of no further evidence. Nor do I know of any evidence for connecting G with Z (I regard the PR reading in 1126—*gyftes*—as an emendation or error; see p. 62). Consequently, either Z, Y_2, and G go back to a common ancestor along independent lines, or G belongs to one line of descent and Y_2 and Z to another. I shall consider the relationship of Y_2 to Z first.

2. Y_2 and Z.

On pages 17-19 I gave a list of readings in which Z appears to be in error and G correct. A few of those readings affect Y_2 also.[35] They are as follows:

1006. Y_2, Z: om. is (A, *evidently emending, reads* is)
1178.   G: if that ȝe rede it me
         Y_2, Z: om. it (M *lacking*)
1217.   G: bestys wilde
         CAS, Y_2: wild(e) bestys (M *lacking*)
         FTB: wilde hertes

To these must be added 1107—an important, but puzzling, line.
(1107.)   G: Of riche beddis & of ornementis
         FTB, S, Y_2:   . . . of pavementȝ (M *lacking*)
         CA (*emending?*)   . . other ornamentes

[35] It is obvious that only Y_2 is affected; for the errors of Y_1 are those of Z.

39

The list is not very long; and the Y_2,Z agreements are not especially striking. The Y_2,Z agreement in 1006 might well be accidental. Either reading is possible in 1178; it is conceivable that G emended the text. The two other cases, however, must be considered carefully.

Editors regard *pavements* (1107) as an error, caught from *parementz* of the preceding line. Skeat says, "I think it clear that this arose from a repetition of the word *parements*, which was afterwards turned to *pavements* by way of desperate emendation. The letters *v* and *r* are often somewhat alike."[36] If Skeat is correct, both Y_2 and Z have the erroneous reading, for CA could have secured *ornamentes* only through an emendation; the alternative is that Y_2, FTB, and S obtained *pavementz* independently, which is unbelievable. If, however, *pavementz* was the original reading, we have to explain the presence of *ornamentes* in CA and G as due to independent emendations or to contamination.

Both words are to be found elsewhere in Chaucer's works: *othere ornementes* in *C.T.* E 258; *pavement* in *C.T.* B 85, B 1867, D 2104, and F 1374. Moreover, one is reminded of the 'paved parlour' of *Troilus*, II. 82, especially as Chaucer is here describing *daunsyng chambres* (1106). The objection to *pavementz* is that one would not speak of a room as 'full of' pavements. On the other hand, one may object to *ornamentes* as being practically a repetition of the idea contained in *parementz*. Considering the ease with which *pavementz* could have crept into the text (as Skeat points out above) and the awkwardness of the phrase 'ful of . . . pavementz,' I should regard G as correct.[37]

In line 1217 the original reading was either *bestys wilde* (G) or *wild(e) bestys* (CAS,Y_2). The other reading—*wilde hertes* —is an error of FTB, influenced perhaps by line 1212. The

[36] Oxford Chaucer, III. 320.

[37] Whichever reading is correct, the CA reading of *other ornamentes* must be regarded as an emendation; for it is evident that Z read *pavementz*. Skeat's argument may be reversed here: it is conceivable that *v* had become *r* in the ancestor of CA, or at least was so read by the scribe of CA; if so, the scribe, not wishing to repeat the word *parementz,* substituted its meaning—*other ornamentes*. Or, *ornamentes* may have crept into CA (and G likewise) through a gloss: *parementz* is an unusual word (Chaucer uses it twice in the *C.T.*, A 2501 and F 269); the word *ornamentes* glossed opposite *parementz* might easily be taken as a correction of *pavementz* in the following line.

true reading must be decided by metrical tests. The line reads in G

> These bestys wilde & han hem at here wille.

In some of the other MSS. final -*e* of *wilde* is dropped, but incorrectly so (ten Brink, 235, 236). Consequently, the reading of Y_2, CAS is

> These wylde bestys and haue theym at theyr wylle.

Bestys is regularly dissyllabic; Chaucer uses it at least ten[38] times elsewhere, and always as a dissyllable. The medial *e(y)* in -*es(-ys)* of *bestys* is very rarely syncopated (ten Brink, 259); moreover, apocope of the final -*e* of an attributive adjective never occurs if the adjective precedes the noun (ten Brink, 236). On the other hand, the order of words in G allows for the elision of final -*e* of *wilde* before the following vowel (ten Brink, 269). Consequently, we are confronted with a choice between the perfectly metrical line of G and one with an extra syllable. Transcriptional probability also favors the G reading; for the poetical order of words—*bestys wilde*— is less likely to be the result of a scribal change than the conversational order.

It must be admitted that the evidence submitted as indicating a connection of Y_2 and Z is not abundant or undebatable. Perhaps the agreement in 1217 indicates that this part of the text belongs to Y_1. The only evidence to the contrary is in line 1235, where G and Y read *hire*, which the rest omit—not very strong evidence. However, meager though the evidence be, I am inclined to accept it as indicating that Y_2 and Z sprang from an ancestor removed by at least one generation from the ancestor of G, Y_2, and Z. Fortunately for the construction of a critical text, it makes but little difference whether Y_2 is independent of Z or not.

3. Readings apparently erroneous in all MSS.

It remains now to consider the readings in which G, Y_2, and Z appear to err together. They are as follows:

903.	G:	That is on graue that we motyn lye
	FTB,M_2:	. . . grave we moten lye
	CA:	. . . graue I-fere we moten ly (A in fere)
	S,f:	. . . graue we mote bothe lye
	P_2:	. . . grave that we to-geder lye

Since the source[39] suggests the idea of "together," one is at

[38] *L.G.W.* 2192; *C.T.* B 3363, C 361, 365, E 201, 572, 683; *P.F.* 86; *R.R.* 895; *H.F.* 936, 965.

[39] See p. 32.

a loss to explain the variant readings. CA is preferable; but its position on the stemma is such that one can explain its reading only as an emendation. Perhaps the line was short, as in FTB,M$_2$, and was emended by the other MSS. With the testimony of Y_2 and Z divided, and the G reading suggestive of an emendation for metre, one is tempted to regard the line as confused or short in a common original.

> 1126. G,F(T)B: Thus can this honurable quene hire gestis calle
> (T: his *for* hire)
> C(A)S: gan *for* can (A *inserts* to *before* calle)
> P$_2$(R$_2$): Thus can this honorable quen her gyftes calle
> (R$_2$: gafe *for* can; all *for* calle)

The line is long in all of the MSS. Y_2 and Z, as well as G, apparently read *can;* for if Chaucer's original read *gan,* three MSS. (G, FTB, and P$_2$) independently changed it to *can* (*gafe* in R$_2$ is a patent emendation). The presence of *gestis* in both G and Z is significant. I regard *gyftes* as a mistake for *geftes* (such a mistake could easily arise) or an emendation. Thus the line is unsatisfactory in all three of the groups of MSS.

> 1210. G,S,T,Th: And forth this noble queen this lady ride
> FB: . . . . . this quene this lady ride
> PR: . . . . . this noble quene doth ryde
> CA: . . . . . thys nobyll quene thus lat I ryde
> (M *lacking*)

The readings which are best authenticated are not grammatical; *ride* (G, S, T, Th, and FB) should be *rideth,* or *rit,* which do not accord with the rime-word—*side.* I believe that CA has in some way—perhaps through a happy guess—recovered the true reading. (See *L.G.W.* 628: *and thus I let hem sayle, L.G.W.* 2382, and *C.T.* A 872-3: *and thus . . . Lete I this noble duc to Atthenes ryde.*) *Ryde* (CA) is the infinitive form.

> 1338. G,F(T)B,Y$_1$: And seyde o swete cloth whil Iuppiter it leste
> C(A)S: *om.* swete

The objection to the line is its length. The source suggests *swete*—

> *Dulces* exuviae, dum fata deusque sinebat.[40]
> (Vergil, *Aeneid* IV. 651)

I regard the hexameter as an oversight of Chaucer's. The poet is imitating his source closely throughout this passage; compare the two lines following with the corresponding lines of the *Aeneid:*

[40] Some MSS. read *sinebant.*

Accipite hanc animan, meque his exsoluite curis;
Vixi, et quem dederat cursum fortuna, peregi.
(*Aen.* IV. 652-3)

Chaucer's lines read thus:

Take now my soul, unbynde me of this unreste;
I have fulfilled of fortune al the cours.

The lines which immediately precede Dido's speech (1336-7), however, are drawn from Chaucer's general knowledge of the story. It is evident, then, that after writing 1336, 1337, and the words *And seyde* of 1338, Chaucer turned to his book to get the gist of Dido's speech; but in returning to his work, he overlooked the value of the measure already written, and added a normal line to it—

O swete cloth whil Iuppiter it leste.

1538.   G: As wolde god that þat I hadde ʒeue
    FTB,CA: *om.* that (2)
        S: *om.* that (2), *but adds* almychti *before* god
        M₁: *om. that* (1, 2)
    (FTBM₁ *reads* y-yive *for* ʒeue)

S and G have emended for metre. It is evident that the line was short in the common original. It is barely possible that Chaucer gave metrical value to a pause—

As wolde God // that I hadde yive.

Such a pause is in keeping with the feigned earnestness of Hercules' praise of Jason. But I think that it is more probable that Chaucer left the line for revision.

1936, 1964. G reads *Thesius* for *Minos.* The other MSS. present the correct name but their verses are weakened by the substitution of the dissyllabic word. In the first case CA normalizes the line by reading *Unto Minos* for *To Minos,* and S by substituting *ffor to* for *To;* in the second case S presents a normal line by reading *King Minos* for *Minos.*

1966. All of the MSS. excepting CA read *Of Athenys* incorrectly. CA emends to *In mochell myrthe,* taking the idea from the second half of the line. (Th reads *Of the towne.*)

Mr. J. L. Lowes has ventured an explanation[41] of this line which is worthy of consideration. He points out an unmistakable influence of Boccaccio's *Teseide* upon this part of the legend of *Ariadne.* He continues, "It is interesting to note that the prison in the *Teseide* which Chaucer seems to have in mind in his description *was* in Athens, so that the reason of the slip may have been his overlooking, for the moment,

[41] *P.L.M.A.,* 20:808n.

43

the fact that in the story he was really telling the scene had been transferred to Crete."[42]

2215.   G: ffor thow so be that boot here ne cone
       M₁: . . . boote here kome
      FTB: . . . botte noon here come
        C: . . . shyp or boot hyr com
     S,Ad: . . . any bote her come
    (A *lacking*)

It is obvious that what Ariadne means to say is that even though a boat should come to the island, she would not dare to return to her country. Consequently, the negative is senseless.[43] The SAd and C readings appear to be emendations.

2422. G,(C)SAd,M₁: And Thetis. Thorus. Triton. & they alle
            FTB: *om.* Triton
            (C: Thora *for* Thorus)

Th has Chorus, which it may have secured from some MS. now lost. Skeat says of this line,[44] "Both Chorus and Thorus are unknown as sea-divinities; but I think I can guess Chaucer's authority, viz., Verg. *Aen.* V. 823-5:

'Et senior Glauci chorus, Inousque Palaemon,
Tritonesque citi, Phorcique exercitus omnis,
Laeua tenent Thetis et Melite, Panopeaque uirgo.'

Here we find *Thetis, chorus, Triton;* whilst 'and they alle' answers to *exercitus omnis.* (So also Bech.)"

In this connection lines 1902 and 1923 should be mentioned also. In both cases Th alone presents the name *Alcathoe* correctly. But since G omits the couplet 1922-3 and has lost the portion of the text containing 1902, one cannot say that the confusion extends beyond Z (Y_2 does not exist).

Two of the lines listed above are objectionable for metrical reasons; 1338 has six measures and 1538 appears to have had but four. (To these could be added a few lines which are somewhat rugged but not positively bad.) For reasons stated

---

[42] If Chaucer was really nodding in this part of the poem, perhaps the reading of *Thesius* in 1936 and 1964 can be ascribed to him too. It is difficult to conceive why G, an unusually careful transcript, should make such an obvious error twice within thirty lines. Besides, when *Minos* is substituted, both lines are headless.

[43] Koch suggests (*Eng. Stud.* 36. 137) that the line be read thus: *For though so be that never boot here come.* In defense of his reading he cites English usage—Koch, Gr. II. §382, and Mätzner, III. 138f. Though both men give many examples of our common idioms 'never so many,' 'never so much,' 'ever so many,' etc., neither gives an example where 'never' *alone* has the force of 'never so many,' etc. Koch's emendation is obviously uncanonical.

[44] Skeat, Oxford Chaucer, III. 344.

above I believe that 1338 was hexametric in Chaucer's own MS.; *swete*—the only superfluous word—was not inserted by a scribe. Likewise, I would disregard the testimony of 1538 and other rugged lines; for though we cannot state positively that these verses were rugged in Chaucer's original, we are pretty safe in assuming that the poet did not leave an unfinished poem of twenty-seven hundred lines without passing over some verses which he expected to recast later.

Of the other lines, 1966 cannot be used as evidence, for *Of Athenys* is very probably Chaucer's own slip. Likewise, 1936 and 1964 must be discarded, for all the MSS. except G read *Minos*, even though their verses are lame; whether the error is one of metre or of the writing *Thesius* for *Minos*, it must be attributed to Chaucer. 1210 and 2422, however, tend to link all the MSS. in error: in the first instance the probably correct reading—that of CA—must be regarded as a happy guess at the truth or as coming from a MS. which stood apart from all existing MSS.; in the second, *Thorus* is very likely a scribe's error, for Th would hardly have emended to *Chorus* without some MS. authority. The testimony of 2422 is weakened, however, by two considerations: (1) the temptation to write the alliterative *Thetis, Thorus, Triton* is so strong and the resemblance of "t" and "c" so close, that the mistake may have been made independently by G and Y_2Z; or (2) Chaucer himself may have made such a change in his working copy[45] (in which case Th had access to an earlier copy of this legend than any which exists today).

Discussion of the other three lines—903, 1126, and 2215— is almost useless. It is conceivable that G has the correct reading in the first instance, but doubtful. 1126 is hopelessly corrupt; the readings do violence to both metre and sense. And in 2215 the best readings appear to be emendations.

G and Y_2Z are further linked in error in that they both omit the 'conclusion' of *Hypermnestra*. The legend breaks off abruptly with these words:

This tale is seid for this conclusion.

[45] In respect to this, note what Lowes has to say about the two versions of the *Prologue* (*P.L.M.A.*, 19. 677). In the early version are verses, phrases, or words, which were taken over almost bodily from the French poems which Chaucer was imitating. Many of these were changed in the later version, after the sources were no longer fresh in the poet's mind; *florouns, e. g.,* becomes *floures*, without a change of meaning.

Each of the other tales has its 'conclusion,' varying from a single couplet to six or seven lines. It is inconceivable that Chaucer did not write the few lines necessary to finish this legend; certainly he would not have put it into circulation in its unfinished state. It is more likely that these lines were written on a separate sheet which became detached from the rest of Chaucer's MS.,—in which case G and Y_2Z are not linked in error by omitting it—or that it was lost from a transcript. The former is the more probable, for Chaucer's MS. was likely a pile of loose leaves; the transcript would probably be a bound up codex.

4. General Conclusions.

At the beginning of this chapter I stated that the two versions of the *Prologue* suggested two types of MSS., which may have descended from Chaucer's MS. in one of three ways —along independent lines; through a common ancestor, removed from Chaucer's original by one or more generations, and containing both forms of the *Prologue;* or one of the two may have been a composite. Our study of the text has shown that the MSS. are divided into two groups, each with its own form of the *Prologue,* and that they are connected in some way by mutual errors. It is obvious that the errors do not point to a composite origin of one of the types, for the errors are fairly well distributed. But whether the mutual errors of G and Y_2Z are from Chaucer's own copy, or from a later manuscript, perhaps cannot be determined beyond doubt.[46] I am inclined to believe that these errors were due to confusion in Chaucer's own MS. For,

I. There are a few cases in which it is pretty certain that Chaucer left verses metrically or logically unsound; such, *e. g.,* are lines 1338 (hexametric) and 1966 (*Of Athenys*). In these two cases we are fortunate in finding sources to prove that the poet nodded. It is not unlikely that other cases exist, for which, however, no evidence can be adduced;

II. Corrections and substitutions written in the margin or

---

[46] In the construction of a critical text it obviously makes little difference whether 'X' is Chaucer's own MS. or a transcript one or more generations removed. In the latter case an editor would regard a corrupt line as a transcriptional error; in the former, a misreading of Chaucer's confused original—his copy would have corrections or substitutions scribbled between the lines and on the margins.

between the lines of Chaucer's working copy would account for some of the imperfect or erroneous readings cited above; the confusion in 1126 and 1210, *e.g.*, may have arisen in just this way;

III. Since 'X' is the source of both G and Y_2Z, it must have had both forms of the *Prologue*. Inasmuch as it is unlikely that any scribe would copy both versions, one is justified in assuming that 'X' is Chaucer's own MS.;

IV. Since the poem was never completed, it is unlikely that Chaucer ever 'published' it;

V. The agreement of G and Y_2Z in the order of legends—though that of the first alone is indicated by the context—and the absence of the 'conclusion' of *Hypermnestra* from both G and Y_2Z can best be explained as independent inheritances from Chaucer's working MS.

In fact, the conclusion toward which all the evidence points is that 'X' was a pile of manuscript in Chaucer's desk drawer at his death, rather than a bound up codex in circulation. Consequently, in drawing my stemma I shall represent G as springing directly from Chaucer's MS. (X), Y_1 as coming from an ancestor of FTB, and Y_2 as probably descending from an ancestor of Z.

The relationship of Th to the MSS.

We are now able to consider the position of Th. It agrees in general with FTB, following that group in such important readings as those of 1139, 1396, 1730, 1736, 1747, 2440, 2491, etc. (see p. 21). But it could not have been derived from FTB altogether: for,

I. It contains every line omitted by FTB except the elusive couplet 960-1. (It omits lines 1326-7, which are present in all of the MSS.)

II. Its readings are frequently correct when those of FTB are wrong. I have not attempted to make a complete list of such readings; but between lines 2000 and 2620 I have noted the following instances:[47]

2003.	FTB:	*om.* hym	
*2008.	"	: asleked *for* achokid	
*2025.	"	: *om.* sarmoun	
*2064.	"	: dede *for* deth	
2080.	"	: *adds* And	

[47] The most important of these FTB errors are listed on p. 21.

*2150^b-3^a.	"	: *om.*

*2150^{b}-3^{a}.	"	: *om.*
*2249.	"	: baste *for* lyst
2319.	"	: of *for* as
2320.	"	: *om.* his
2404.	"	: *om.* is
*2498.	"	: *om.* mot
2504.	"	: *om.* hid
2555.	"	: *om.* sent
2592.	"	: *om.* what
*2615.	"	: *om.* of soun
*2619.	"	: *om.* ryght

III. In a few instances it combines the readings of FTB (or FTBY_1) with those of G,CAS. The most notable instance is in line 2338, where Th preserves the original reading and presents the spurious line of FTBM_1 as well. In line 1172 Th reads *ilke newe* for *ilke* of FTB and *newe* of G,CAS,Y_2, although it does violence to the metre in so doing. And in 2452 Th (and C) read *queene Phillis* instead of *quene* (FTB) or *Philes* (G,SAd,M_1).

In a few instances Th has the correct reading when M_1 agrees with FTB in error; I have noted but three, and these three occur in the same part of the text—2592, 2615, and 2619 (see above). In two cases Th alone has the correct reading— *Alcathoe* (1902, 1023), and *Chorus* (2422); these may be emendations or they may have been secured from some MS. no longer existing. In 1721 Th reads *Livi* for *our boke;* Th has probably taken a marginal gloss. In 1727 Th agrees with G in reading *so long* for *to long,* and in 831 with G and P_2 in reading *herte* for *heere;* both agreements may be accidental. Sometimes Th agrees with T rather than with FTB; in 1736, *e. g.,* Th and T read *heuynesse,* FB *hevytee,* the other MSS. (correctly) *honeste.*

But one conclusion can be drawn from the above facts, *viz.,* that Thynne drew his text mainly from an FTB MS. but had at his command one or more MSS. from which he corrected many of the FTB errors. With the exception of a very few readings (see above—831, 1727, 1902, 1923, 2242), Th can be constructed from the Z group of MSS.

I submit the following graphic representation of the conclusions reached in the foregoing discussion:

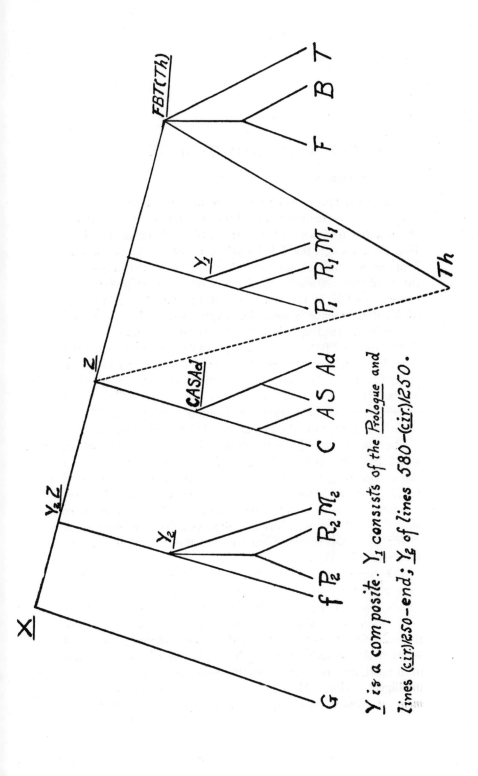

X

G   f P₂ R₂M₂   C A S Ad   P₁ R₁M₁   F B T

Y₂Z   Z   Y₁

CASAd   Th

Y₂   FBT(Th)

Y is a composite. Y₁ consists of the *Prologue* and
lines (cir.)1250–end; Y₂ of lines 580–(cir.)1250.

CHAPTER III

THE SKEAT AND GLOBE TEXTS

1. *Introduction.*

If my conclusions concerning the kinship of the MSS. are correct, it is evident that an editor who gives great weight to the isolated testimony of F (or FTB) is doing so unwisely. For, even though the FTB reading is metrically or logically superior to those of the other MSS., if it is contradicted by the combined testimony of G and CASAd, it is probably incorrect; and if to the testimony of G,CASAd is added that of M, the evidence is overwhelmingly against the correctness of the FTB reading. If, in spite of the evidence, one still thinks that FTB has the only acceptable reading, one must regard it merely as a successful emendation or as having come from Chaucer's MS. through a line of descent independent of that of FTB as a whole. But to choose an FTB reading in preference to an equally good one of the other MSS., as Gl and Sk frequently do, is unwarranted and unscholarly.

The conclusions of the foregoing chapter also show that M, which has been practically ignored by both Gl and Sk, is a manuscript of great authority. When it stands outside of Z (as M_2), it can settle a controversy between G and Z; when it stands within Z (as M_1), its value is two-fold; it may agree with CASAd against FTB and thus establish the reading of Z; or it may present an earlier, and thus truer, reading of FTB (as $FTBM_1$).

My stemma proves also that the confidence which editors have placed in G has been well founded. Inasmuch as G stands alone, it has great weight; but, on the other hand, its very uniqueness offsets to some extent its authority, because its readings cannot be checked. One cannot always tell whether the smoothness of the metre is due to a preservation of the original reading or to the mending of the text by an intelligent scribe. Miss Hammond states that in the *Parlement of Foules,* where G can be checked, the G scribe has normalized several headless lines and smoothed out the metre of many others by omissions or insertions.[1] The G text of *Troilus,* on the other hand, shows very little 'editing' of an intelligent sort; Dr. Root states that the scribe frequently omitted "a word not necessary to the sense, to the utter confusion of the metre."[2] It is probable, then, that the 'editing' of the G text of *P.F.* was due not to the G scribe, but to his exemplar.

Miss Hammond's characterization of the G text of *P.F.* would not apply to that of the *Legend;* for though many of the lines of the latter are not above suspicion of having been 'edited' (*e.g.* 725, 2480), large numbers of them are headless or somewhat rugged. Of the twenty-six lines from *L.G.W.* cited by Skeat (Oxford Chaucer, III. xlv, xlvi) as examples of headless lines, all but two are headless in G, and those two (67 and 111) have undergone revision at the hands of the poet. Six of the twenty-six have been 'edited' by one or more of the other scribes. To Skeat's list could be added several more; G alone presents 1449 as a headless line, and 2471 in G is octosyllabic. In general, then, I take the readings of G at face value, though keeping an eye open for corrections and erasures in the MS. But between a reconstructed reading of Y_2Z (or of Z where Y_2 does not exist) and an equally good one of G, I incline to the former; for the reconstructed Y_2Z is pure, whereas G cannot be checked. Usually G agrees with the reconstructed Y_2Z, thus increasing my confidence in G. Note, for instance, how the reading of Y_2Z can be determined in 641 and 1659; in each case G verifies the reconstructed reading.

Of the other MSS. I need say but little further; their positions on the stemma indicate pretty clearly the degree of their authority. The habits of some of them to emend for metre and sense, and of others to disregard (apparently) both, have been discussed and illustrated in the foregoing pages. I need only add that in trying to determine the true readings in the following lines I have kept constantly in mind the characteristics of the MSS. as well as the value of their positions on the stemma.

[1] Univ. of Chicago, Decennial Publs., *Text of Chaucer's Parlement of Foules,* VII. pp. 24-5.
[2] *The Textual Tradition of Chaucer's Troilus* (Chaucer Soc. Publs., First Series, XCIX), p. 13.

In approaching this work I have tried, furthermore, to set aside all preconceived notions of Chaucerian metre. If the evidence points unmistakably to a headless line, I accept it as Chaucer's, in spite of ten Brink's skepticism[3]; and if, after making all reasonable allowance for error, I find that the MSS. support a line of four or of six feet, I refuse to reject or reconstruct it. For, after all, our knowledge of Chaucer's skill in handling verse can come only from the MSS.; and, moreover, it is not unreasonable to suppose that a poet—even one of the greatest—would leave a number of rugged lines in an unfinished poem of twenty-seven hundred lines.

2. *Erroneous or doubtful readings in the Skeat and Globe texts.*

    1. Sk: A thousand tymes have I herd men telle   CAS
       Gl: A thousande tymes I have herd . . .   T(FB)

(FB, P_1 *om.* men; P_1 I *inserted above, later;* B sithes *for* tymes; G have I herd; sythis *for* tymes.

The evidence of the MSS. is equally divided. Transcriptional probability favors *have I herd,* because *I have herd* is the language of the scribe's daily life. Moreover, the testimony of G ought to be given some weight; for *sythes* may very well be a scribal reading (note B); and there is no good reason for supposing that *have I* of G represents a revised reading and that the G,CAS agreement is due to coincidence. I should accept the CAS reading as that of both versions.

    5. Sk: That ther nis noon S,(G),FTBP,(—F)
      Gl: That ther is noon   CA,F

(G ne is *for* nis)

The testimony of the MSS. cannot always be taken at face value in cases such as this, for the negative particle is so easily omitted or inserted. Moreover, individual characteristics of scribes can easily creep into such lines; one scribe may naturally contract the particle with the verb following, another write it separate, and still another clip it altogether. Thus, my collation reveals a tendency on the part of FTB to contract the particle when it precedes a copulative or auxiliary verb—*nys, nam, nas,* etc.; G more often keeps the particle distinct—*ne is, ne am,* etc.; CA, and less frequently CASAd, often omit it. In this section I give a list of all the

[3] *Language and Metre of Chaucer,* pp. 215-6.

lines in which Sk and Gl differ regarding the particle, and the readings of the MSS., but I do not attempt to decide upon the true reading.

> 6. Sk: That either hath in heven or helle y-be   S
> Gl: . . . . or in helle y-be   FTBP$_1$
> (A in hevyn or in hell hath be; C in helle of heuyn be; G in helle or heuene I-be)

The agreement of C with G and the transposition of *hath* in A suggest confusion in CA. Moreover, the ease with which *in* (2) could creep into the line and the slight roughness which it gives the line indicates that FTBP$_1$ is in error. I believe that S preserves the reading of Z.

> 40. Sk and Gl: Now have I than swich (suche) a condicioun   FB
> (P$_1$ eke a *for* swich a; T eke; CA eke thys; S lo thys; G this, *but reads* therto *for* than)

The only authority for *swich a* is FB. With T,P$_1$, and CA reading *eke,* and G supporting them with *therto,* I conclude that *eke* was the reading of Z. The reading of Z must have been *thanne eke a* (FTBP$_1$) or *then eke thys* (CAS). The *this* of G suggests the latter—a perfectly logical reading.

> 129 (117).[4] Sk and Gl: That naked was, and clad hit new agayn   FB
> (T in *for* hit; S him; CA hem; P *om.;* G And clothede hym in grene al newe a-geyn)

The *hit* (*yt*) of FB may be an attempt to make sense of the FTB reading *in.* Z undoubtedly read *him.* Chaucer is using the personal pronouns *his* and *him* in referring to the earth and winter in the preceding lines. The reading of G (though revised) supports *him.*

> 131 (119).[4] Sk: That from the panter   G,CAS
> Gl: That of the panter   FTBP$_1$

Since there is no reason to believe that the reading of G is due to a revision, I should accept the authority of G,CAS as conclusive.

> 141 (129). Sk: In worshipinge and preisinge   S,P$_1$
> Gl: In worshipynge and in preysing   FTB
> (C in worshyp and praysyng; G,A in worschepe & in preysyng)

---

[4] The numbers in parentheses refer to the corresponding lines in G. A dash within parenthesis (—) indicates that G has no reading corresponding.

The testimony of the MSS. is so badly confused that the true reading cannot be determined. I am more ready to believe that the reading of G and A was the original reading of both versions than that the reading of G is a revision. The -*ing* could easily attach itself to *worship* when a scribe is 'dictating' to himself as he writes.

164 (—).⁴ Sk: But I ne clepe nat innocence folye   A
        Gl: But I ne clepe it innocence folye

(FTBP₁ But I ne clepe yt nat Innocence folye; C *om.* yt nat; A *om.* yt; S that *for* yt nat)

S apparently supports the reading *yt,* for *that* (*þt*) and *yt* are easily confused. Yet *yt* cannot be justified by the context. It seems clear that FTBP₁ preserves the erroneous reading of *Z*, and that the rest emended or stumbled. Since the line does not occur in G, the true reading cannot be determined.

185 (—). Sk: That wel by reson men hit calle may   CAS,T,P₁
       Gl: That men by resoun wel it calle may   FB

Gl takes an inferior arrangement of the words upon the single authority of FB. It is evident that the Sk reading must have been that of *Z*.

191 (75). Sk and Gl: For as to me nis lever   FB(T)(P₁)
(G,CA(S) is *for* nis)
See discussion of line 5.

192 (76). Sk and Gl: I nam with-holden   FTB
(G,CAS I am witholde; P₁ I am not)
Cf. 191 and see l. 5.

196 (80). Sk and Gl: er swich thing   FTBP₁
(G,CAS er swich strif)

G agrees with CAS except in the position of the line. But as the G passage as a whole has been revised to fit into its new position, the authority of G is proportionately weakened, even though it cannot be proved that this particular line underwent revision. It is hardly conceivable, however, that a scribe would change the colorless word *thing* to the more definite *strif.* Consequently, we are shut up to the alternatives of accepting *strif* as the reading of *Z*, or of regarding its presence in CAS as the result of contamination from the revised *Prologue.* The second of these alternatives must be dismissed because of lack of evidence of such contamination—this and 404 are the only important cases in which FTBP$_1$ is not *clearly* in error; the first can be more easily accepted because of the occurrence of *thing* in the preceding line, and the consequent probability of the FTBP$_1$ scribe's catching the word from the line he had just written. So I should follow CAS, regarding *strif* as the reading of both versions of the *Prologue*.[5]

211 (—). Sk: that I so love and dredde CAS
      Gl: that I love so and dredde FTBP$_1$

The authority of the MSS. is equally divided; the choice of readings resolves itself into a determination of Chaucerian usage. Upon the basis of inherent probability I should say that the Sk reading is decidedly preferable; for it allows the accent to fall upon the important word *love* rather than upon *so,* and it allows for the elision of final *-e* before the vowel in *and.*

261 (215). Sk and Gl: that hast of love swich peyne FTBP$_1$
(G,CAS for love)

The evidence of the MSS. favors *for love. For,* in the sense of "because of," fits the context perfectly. Perhaps FTBP$_1$ caught *of love* from the preceding line.

314 (240). Sk: And seyde, 'sir, hit am I' G,C(A)S,T,P$_1$
      Gl: And seyde, 'It am I' FB

Gl omits *sir* upon the single authority of FB.[6] Not only is the manuscript evidence overwhelmingly in favor of the politer form of address, but the poet's subsequent speeches to the God of Love also favor it. (See 319 and 505.)

336 (314). Sk and Gl: For, thogh that thou reneyed hast my lay C,S
(FTBP$_1$ For thogh thou; A ffor though thou haste rememberyd my laye; G Althow thow reneyist hast myn lay)

The authority for *that* rests upon C and S independently or, perhaps, upon C(A)S. The reading of *that* gives a smoother line metrically; but with both G and FTBP$_1$ clipping the first foot, I am inclined to regard the C,S reading as an emendation[7]—probably independent C and S emenda-

---

[5] Lowes overlooks the CAS reading in referring to this line in his argument for the priority of the 'B version' of the *Prologue*. (See *P.M.L.A.,* 19. 664.)

[6] In line 1706 FB makes a somewhat similar mistake.

[7] Line 2359 presents a similar case. C and S (A text lost) read *For that by that the yeer,* while the other MSS. omit *that* (2).

tions, for A gets a metrical line by another emendation. Consequently, I should place this line with the list of Chaucer's headless lines.

404 (390). Sk and Gl: with a dredful herte   FTBP₁
(G,(CA)S with a sorweful herte—CA *adds* ryght *before* sorweful)

I should accept *sorweful* because of the combined authority of G,CAS. *Dredful* may have suggested itself to the FTBP₁ scribe as a synonymous reading for *sorweful*.

415 (403). Sk: Yet hath he maked lewed folk delyte   (G)
Gl: . . . . he made lewde folke delyte   FTB(P₁),C(A)S
(G He hath *for* Yet hath he: to *before* delyte; A to *before* delyte; P Yet he hath: men *for* folk)

Sk rejects *made* of Z for metrical reasons;[8] Gl here and elsewhere recognizes *made* as a dissyllable. Ten Brink says, "Where *made* occurs as a dissyllable, either *maked* or *maden* should be read."[9]

449 (439). Sk: doth with him as yow leste   FTB,C
Gl: dooth with hym what yow liste   G,S,A,P₁

For reasons stated on p. 38 I regard the Gl reading as correct.

461 (451). Sk: That han me holpe and put in this degree CAS,B,(P₁)
Gl: . . . . and put me in this degree F,T,(G)
(P *om.* and put; G swich *for* this; holpyn *for* holpe)

The second *me* was probably the reading of Z as well as of G; CAS and B dropped it for metre—P by mistake.

557 (—). Sk: Have hem now in thy Legend alle in minde   M₁,T
Gl: Have hem in thy Legende now . . . . .   FB
(CA Haue now in thy legend hem al; S,P₁ Haue thame in thy legend al)

Since M₁ and T both contradict FB, and P₁ is non-committal, I believe that M₁ and T preserve the reading of FTBY₁. The reading of the other branch of Z—CAS—is not so easy to determine. Combining the readings of CA and S, however, gives *Haue hem now*, which is the reading of FTBY₁. I should accept the Sk reading, then, as having the greater weight of probability in its favor. (Chaucer uses *legende*

---

[8] In the 1889 edition Sk gets a metrical line by reading *he made the lewed folk*, though he has no authority for *the*.
[9] *Language and Metre of Chaucer*, p. 173, F. N.

at times with the accent on the first syllable and at times on the second. Skeat records five other instances of the use of the word in Chaucer—*C.T.* A 3141, B 1335, 4311; *L.G.W.* 438, 2456. In the first three cases the word occurs in the middle of the line and is accented upon the first syllable; in the last two cases at the end of the line and accented on the last syllable. In the Sk reading above the accent is according to usage.)

560 (—). Sk: Than thou knowest, that been good wommen alle S
        Gl: . . . . . . and ben good wommen alle.
(*For* that been good wommen, CA *reads* and good women, FTBP₁ good wommen, M₁ goode wommen)

The CAS reading is doubtful; *been* has the authority of a single MS.—one which frequently emends for metre. CA probably preserves the reading of CAS, though it may have dropped *been*. It is preferable to accept the perfectly clear, satisfactory reading of $FTBP_1M_1$—*goode wommen alle; goode,* the plural form of the adjective, is dissyllabic (ten Brink, 232); the fact that M_1 alone retains the *-e* indicates merely that most scribes of the fifteenth century failed to understand fully the value of the inflectional ending.[10] (This should be added to the list of headless lines.)

587. Sk: unto her obeisaunce G
      Gl: at hir obeysaunce FTB,M₂,S
(CA vnder theyr obeysance; P₂ at her plesaunce)

The evidence of the MSS. favors the Gl reading; perhaps G was influenced by *unto* in the preceding line. The Gl reading necessitates a quadrisyllabic value for *obeysaunce,* a value which it also has in 1375 (S and P only disagreeing).

603. Sk: Him thoughte, nas to him no thing so due (G)
      Gl: Him thoghte ther was nothing to him so due (*Rest*)
(G there nas to hym; C *om.* so)

Sk drops *there* from G for metrical reasons; since it appears in every MS., I should accept it, regarding *thought(e)* as monosyllabic. Whether G or Y_2Z is correct in the order of words cannot be determined. As regards the absence of the negative particle from Y_2Z, see line 5.

622. Sk: And forthy to theffect (G),S,(A),B,(P₂)
      Gl: . . . . to effect F,T,C

[10] In this respect M is an exceptionally good transcript. See line 1391 (p. 18) for a similar instance.

(G thefeect *for* theffect; A forthe then *for* forthy; P₂ þer *for* forthy; M *lacking*)

The MSS. indicate that the article should be retained.

623. Sk: I wol lete hit slippe   FTB,C
     Gl: I wol lete slyppe   G,A
(S will I lat ourslip; P *and* M *lacking*)

Hit is awkwardly intrusive; it got into FTB and C as separate emendations for metre, I believe (note that S emends also). G and A rightly recognized the dissyllabic value of *lete*.

641. Sk and Gl: Among the ropes, and the shering-hokes   FTB
(*For* and, S *reads* than; A rafe[11]; C raf; P₂ thenn; Th ran; G rennyth; M *lacking*)

Gl and Sk are clearly wrong. *Z* Evidently read *ran*, which Th preserves (thus contradicting FTB) and CA bungled to *raf;* S mistook r(r) for the somewhat similar th(þ). P₂ made a like mistake, converting *renneþ* (perhaps *renneþ þe* had become *renne þe* in the exemplar of P₂) of $Y_2 Z$ into *thenn.* This reconstructed reading *(rennyth)* of Y_2Z is also the reading of G; the tense is consistent with the context. The corrected text reads thus:

> In goth the grapenel so ful of crokes;
> Among the ropes rennyth the shering-hokes.

Professor Schofield has pointed out[12] that "grapenel" was a contrivance for lashing ships together (not for "clutching ropes," as Skeat states in his notes to this line). Thus Froissart, writing of the English victory of Sluys, states,[13] "In order to be more successful, they had *large grapnels, and iron hooks with chains,* which they flung from ship to ship, to moor them to each other." (I. 209) (See Schofield's paper for two other similar passages from Froissart.) Professor Schofield would have greatly strengthened his point if he had consulted the MSS. instead of accepting Skeat's reading as authentic; for it is evident that the "grapenel so ful of crokes" does not go "among the ropes."

670. Sk and Gl: That ther nis tonge noon that may hit telle   FTB
(G,S is tunge non; CA,(P₂) is no tung; M *lacking*)

[11] The Chaucer Society print reads *rase* (wrongly).
[12] W. H. Schofield, *The Sea-battle in Chaucer's 'Legend of Cleopatra'* (Anniversary Papers by Colleagues and Pupils of George Lyman Kittredge), p. 147.
[13] See *Ibid.*

The MSS. indicate that *is* is correct. But see line 5.

725. Sk and Gl: And Tisbe hight the maid, Naso seith thus   G
(*The other MSS. om.* And)

Since the evidence of the MSS. is equally divided, one is not able to determine definitely the true reading. But one should hold in mind the fact that G may have normalized the line. I prefer the headless line, because I think the pause is very effective.

750. Sk: Upon that o syde   G,M$_2$,f,T,B,CAS
    Gl: Upon the o syde   F,P$_2$

G,Y_2, and Z evidently read *that*. Though it is possible that *that* was caught from the following line, it is hardly possible that it was so caught by so many scribes independently.

788. Sk: And faste by this grave Y_2,Z
    Gl: And faste by his grave
(G there *for* this)

Not a single MS. reads *his;* perhaps Gl misprints.

794. Sk and Gl: And so greet lyking Piramus to see   Z
(G,P$_2$,f haste *for* lyking)

This reading has been discussed on p. 39. *Lykynge* is probably an error of Z.

816. Sk: And thus she sit   G,Y_2,Z
    Gl: And ther she sytte

All the MSS. read *thus*. The Gl emendation is entirely uncalled for.

825. Sk and Gl: The mone shoon, men mighte wel y-see   FTB
(G & *for* men; (CA)S,M$_2$P$_2$f and he *for* men)

I regard *men* as an FTB emendation. Y_2Z evidently read *and he,* which is probably the correct reading; *he* dropped out of G. The final *-e* of *mighte* may be regarded as mute (ten Brink, 261).

837. Sk: My bidding hath yow slain, as in this cas   G
    Gl: My byddyng hath i-slayn yow in this caas   P$_2$
(*Rest follow G in word order but om.* as; CA sory *for* this)

Gl is clearly wrong. Whether G is correct *(as in this cas)* or Y_2Z *(in this cas)* is not easy to determine. Y_2Z is metrical if the participle be read as a dissyllable [ten Brink allows the form *slawen* (149) but not *slayen* (196)]. However, I incline to G; this almost pleonastic use of *as* is fairly common in Chaucer—*as in, as by, as after,* etc. (Cf. *as in this cas, C.T.* B 123, 305; *as in his tyme, C.T.* B 3688, 3744.) One cannot determine whether the second word should be *bidding* (command) or *biding* (delay). G,FTBTh, and C write the word with two *d*'s, M_2P_2f, S, and A with one.[14] Perhaps the difference in spelling did not signify to the scribes a difference in meaning. Line 838 indicates that *bidding* is correct.

880. Sk: O spek, my Piramus   G,CAS,M_2f(P_2)
     Gl: O speke, Piramus   FTB
(P_2 my love Pyramus)

The authority of the MSS. is overwhelmingly in favor of the Sk reading. Moreover, *spek,* rather than *speke,* is the form of the singular imperative of the strong verb.

890. Sk: My woful hand   f
     Gl: Thy woful hand   *(Rest)*
(G myn, *written over an erased* thy *by a contemporary hand*)

The source of this passage demands *my*—

> "Tua te manus, inquit, amorque
> Perdidit, infelix. *Est et mihi fortis in unum*
> *Hoc manus:"*   (Ovid, *Met.* iv. 147-9.)

But f alone has the obviously correct reading. I believe that *thy* is Chaucer's own slip, corrected in an early MS.—perhaps Chaucer's original—from which the exemplar of f and the corrector of G got *my(n)*. *Woful* also suggests that Chaucer began by translating *Tua * * * manus * * * infelix,* though he took the rest of the clause from the next sentence of Ovid.[15]

903. Sk and Gl: That in o grave y-fere we moten lye   CA

See p. 41 for the variant readings and for a discussion of this line. I should print the CA reading, but only as a successful emendation of a bad, or doubtful, reading.

911. Sk: Been as trewe and loving   G,FTB,M_2f
     Gl: Ben also trewe and lovynge (A)
(C as trew in *for* as trewe and; S als trewe in; A also trewe in; P_2 as trow of)

[14] M reads *bydynge,* not *hydynge* as the Chaucer Society print records.
[15] Gl suggests that perhaps a couplet has fallen out. If so, the missing lines stood between 890 and 891. That would imply that four successive lines were in rime or that *quod she* stood originally in the third line of Thisbe's speech. Both are very unlikely.

Gl takes the reading of A, substituting *and* for *in* (the reading of CAS). The only apparent reason for accepting this minor authority is that of avoiding a headless line. The headless line is clearly correct.

952. Sk: as wolde destinee   FTB,S
     Gl: as wolde his destanee   G,CA,$M_2P_2R_2$

The evidence of the MSS. favors the Gl reading. Its metre is as good as that of the alternative reading, since the *-e* of *wolde* regularly elides before the following initial *h* (ten Brink, 269). Chaucer sometimes speaks of *Destiny* as being synonymous with the name *Wirdes* (*L.G.W.* 2580), or Fates. But by far his more common use of the word is as an abstract noun—my destiny, his destiny, a blisful destiny, etc. (See *L.G.W.* 1299; *C.T.* A 1842, 2322; *T.C.* II. 1091, III. 734, V. 1108.) Thus both usage and the evidence of the MSS. support the Gl reading.

994. Sk: And shortly tolde him al the occasioun G,M_2(P_2R_2),CAS
     Gl: *om.* him   FTB
(P_2R_2 hem *for* him)

The Sk reading has the authority of the MSS. and is better metrically; for it allows for the elision of final *-e* of *tolde* before initial *h* (ten Brink, 269) and for the usual combination of *the* and the first syllable of *occasioun* (ten Brink, 270).

1053. Sk and Gl: The quene, and of her socour her beseke   FTB
(G,S,$M_2P_2R_2$ to *for* her (2); (CA) that ys so meke *for* to beseke)

I regard *to* as correct. *Her* is the indirect object after *of,* though the FTB and CA scribes regarded it as a possessive modifying *socour* and emended their texts accordingly.

1091. Sk: her messageres go   FB
     Gl: hire messagers to go   T,C,S,(R_2)
(G,A,M_2,P_2 for to go; R_2 anon to goo)

Manuscript evidence counts for little in such a line, for the scribes were very free in using *to* and *for to*. Sk follows FB to get an exact decasyllabic line, giving the plural ending of *messageres* syllabic value. But the MSS. support the sign of the infinitive, though one cannot tell whether *to* or *for to* is correct.

1094. Sk: She many a beste to the shippes sente   (G)
     Gl: Ful many a beeste she to the shippes sente
                                FTB,(CAS),($M_2P_2R_2$)

(CAS,M₂,P₂ his *for* the; P₂R₂ Full mony a best to his (R *om.* to his) shippes she sent; G Sche manye a beste sche to the shippis sente—*the second* sche *being scratched out*)

In defense of his reading Sk says that all the MSS. except G wrongly read *beest, she* for *beste* (Oxford Chaucer, III. 122). Such an explanation, though ingenious, is uncalled for. The position of *she* in each of the three lines following indicates that Gl has taken the correct reading.

1099. Sk: He never beter at ese was his lyve   FB,S
      Gl: He never better at ese was in his lyve   T,C(A),M₂P₂R₂
(G He nevere at ese was betyr in al hese lyve *but* betyr in al hese lyve *is in a later hand over an erasure;*[16] A For *for* He; he *before* in)

Skeat's omission of *in* lacks the support of the best MSS. and of good M. E. usage. The alternative reading is metrically sound, since the final weak -*e* of *ese* may be considered mute (ten Brink, 261).

1107. Sk and Gl: Of riche beddes, and of ornaments   G
(CA other ornamentes; FTB,S,P₂R₂ pavementz; M *lacking*)
See p. 40 for a discussion of this line.

1109. Sk and Gl: And with the quene whan that he had sete   FTB
(*Rest om.* that)

FTB evidently emended for metre. The other scribes either read the line as four-stressed or considered *hadde* dissyllabic. The latter is quite possible; ten Brink remarks—270 (2)— that *hadde* (A. S. *haefde*) is sometimes dissyllabic even when an initial *h* follows it. In the *L.G.W.* there are several lines which require that the final -*e* of *hadde* be given syllabic value (see 215, 1488, 1537).

1126. Sk: Thus can this [noble] quene her gestes calle
      Gl: Thus gan this queene honoure hir gestes talle
(G,FTB Thus can this honurable quene hire (T his) gestis calle; CAS gan *for* can; A to call; P₂R₂ gyftes *for* gestis; R₂ gafe *for* can; all *for* calle; M *lacking*)

Both Sk and Gl have attempted to reconstruct this line, which is too long in all the MSS. The best authenticated reading is that of G,FTB; for *gyftes* (PR) is pretty certainly a mistake or emendation of Y_2, and *gan* of CAS—*gafe* (R) is obviously an emendation. Gl reconstructs the line from the MSS., suggesting *honoure* for *honorable* and the compli-

---

[16] Not recorded in the Chaucer Society print.

mentary epithet *talle* for *calle* ("t" and "c" were frequently confused). Sk suggests *noble queene* because it is a common Chaucerian phrase (see 1143, 1210, 1222). Chaucer's sources for this legend give no clue to the reading of the line. Judging by the context the line ought to mean 'Thus, her guests have every reason to call this queen honorable.' Perhaps Chaucer left it thus:

Thus cán this quén honoráble hir géstes cálle.

In the preceding chapter I have listed this line with a few others which were probably unsatisfactory in Chaucer's own MS.

1145. Sk and Gl: I make of hit no cure FTB
(G,CAS,P_2R_2 take *for* make; M *lacking*)

I accept *take* on the basis of manuscript evidence and Chaucerian usage. *Cure* (O. F. *cure*, L. *cura*) means "heed," "care," "attention." Hence, *I take of it no cure* means "I take no heed of it," "I pay no attention to it' (see *N.E.D.* *cure*), which is obviously Chaucer's meaning. So too in *C.T.* B 4200, *L.G.W.* 1906. I cannot find *make of it no cure* elsewhere in Chaucer's works.

1172. Sk and Gl: This ilke Troyan FTB
(G,CAS,P_2R_2 newe *for* ilke; M *lacking*)

Newe is obviously correct. (Cf. 1151 *thise newe lusty folke of Troye*.)

1178. Sk: Now certes, Anne, if that ye rede hit me G
Gl: . . . . . gif that ye rede me FTB,(C)AS,(P_2R_2)
(C,P_2R_2 *om.* that)

Both forms are metrically correct. Though the evidence of the MSS. is balanced, I should adopt the Z reading; for *hit* is more likely to be intrusive than to drop out.

1187. Sk and Gl: for no wight Z
(G,$M_2P_2R_2$ thing *for* wight)

This line has been discussed on p. 39. I accept *thing* because evidence for a G,Y_2 relationship is almost negligible.

1202. Sk and Gl: And she is fair, as is the brighte morwe F(T)B
(M *lacking;* rest as *for* is (1); T *om.* is (2); G bright *for* faire)

Chaucer's original probably read *as for is* (1); for the change from *as* to *is* is the natural one (since the verb is required in prose) and a change from *is* to *as* could have been made only by G,PR, and CAS independently. It cannot be determined whether G errs in reading *bright* for *faire* or whether Y_2Z emended; I am inclined to believe that G is in error, the scribe having 'anticipated' *bright* as he 'dictated' the line to himself. (Anticipation of the coming word would explain the G readings of 1094 and 1370 also.)

1210. Sk: And forth this noble quene thus lat I ryde   CA
     Gl: And forth this noble queene, this lady, ride   G,FTB,S
(P_2R_2 queene doth ryde; M *lacking*)

Gl prints the G,FTB,S line without comment. But it is hardly fair to accuse Chaucer of writing a form which apparently did not exist in M. E.—*ride* should be *rideth.* On the other hand, the CA reading can be regarded only as an emendation, though a clever and successful one. It is in accordance with Chaucer's usage (see *L.G.W.* 628: *and thus I let hem sayle; C.T.* A 872-3: *And thus * * * Lete I this noble duc to Atthenes ryde*) ; and it is grammatical, *ryde* being the infinitive. I should accept it, either as a clever guess of the scribe's, or as coming from an excellent authority now lost.

1215. Sk: That I mighte ones mete him with this spere   CAS,P_2(R_2)
     Gl: That I myght hym ones meten with this spere G,FTB
(R a *for* this; M *lacking*)

It is evident that the agreement of either G,FTB or of CAS,PR is the result of accident. One must determine the reading upon the basis of metre. Of the two the Sk reading is preferable; for the *-e* of *mete* regularly elides before *hym* (ten Brink, 269), and the order of words allows the accent to fall upon *ónes* and *méte.* The alternative reading is rugged.

1217. Sk: These hertes wilde
     Gl: The wilde hertes   FTB
(CAS These wyld bestys; P_2R_2 The wilde bestys; G These bestys wilde; M *lacking*)

Sk and Gl are clearly wrong in accepting *hertes,* for both CAS and P_2R_2 contradict FTB; it is evident that Y_2Z read *wilde bestys.* Between that reading and the one of G, *bestys wilde,* I should choose the latter, for it allows for the elision of final *-e* of *wilde* and for the dissyllabic value of *bestys,* and because transcriptional probability favors the poetical order of words (see my argument on pp. 40-1).

It is less easy to determine whether *The* or *These* is cor-

64

rect. Probability slightly favors *These:* for PR is very erratic in minor particulars; *These* fits the context better, referring backward definitely; and FTB has already been convicted of one transgression in this line. I should accept, then, *These bestys wilde.*

1235. Sk and Gl: and chaunge for no newe   *Z*
(G,P$_2$R$_2$ and chaunge hire for; M *lacking*)

Since the final -*e* of *chaunge* elides regularly before *hire* (ten Brink, 269), either reading is possible. I should accept the combined evidence of G,PR, though holding in mind the ease with which the pronoun could have been inserted by the scribes.

1238. Sk: And took him for husband, [to been] his wyf
    Gl: . .   . . . . and became his wife *(All MSS.)*
(G,S,A,P$_2$ become *for* became; R$_2$ her *before* husband)

Sk emends because the line cannot be scanned. Chaucer probably left the line imperfect as it occurs in the MSS.

1273. Sk: Noot I nat what   G,S,T,M$_1$
    Gl: Wot I not what   FB,P$_1$
(CA But *for* Noot)

The MSS. favor the Sk reading. But see line 5.

1285. Sk: that hath so depe   G,S
    Gl: that hath thus depe   FTB,CA
(P$_1$R$_1$ was so *for* hath so; M *lacking*)

I should accept the Sk reading, partly on the authority of the MSS., for G is supported by S and *Y$_1$* (which belongs to *Z*); and partly because transcriptional probability favors it, since the scribe is more likely to combine the -*th* of *hath* with the following *so* than to write *so* for *thus.*

1319. Sk: And, so ye wil me now to wyve take
                              G,C,S,(T,B,M$_1$),(P$_1$),(R$_1$)
    Gl: . . . .   . now me . .   (F),(A)
(G,CAS *alone read* so)

Gl follows F blindly. The alternative reading is smoother, as well as better authenticated.

1330. Sk: Thus hath he laft Dido in wo and pyne (G)
    Gl: And thus he lefte Dido in wo and pyne C(A)S,(P$_1$R$_1$)
(G Thus he hath; FTB And thus hath he; M$_1$ And thus hath CAS,P$_1$R$_1$ And thus he; A in *before* pyne; P$_1$R$_1$ sorrow *for* wo)

All the MSS. except G read *And thus;* G reads *Thus.* The presence of *And* makes the line too long—*And thus hath he left*—as FTB reads it. To obviate this difficulty M omits *he,* and CAS,PR *hath.* Because of these efforts to mend the line, I think that *And* is intrusive. So I reject the Gl line. Sk follows G in omitting *And,* and FTB in word-order. But G presents a perfectly good reading—*Thus he hath left.* Acting upon the principle of not emending the text when an excellent authority has a desirable reading, I accept G rather than Sk. The G line, with an inverted accent, is not a whit less desirable than that of Sk.

> 1338. Sk: And seide, 'O cloth, whyl Iupiter it leste'   C(A)S
>   Gl: And seyde, 'O swete cloth, while [Jove] hit leste'
> (*Rest* And seyde o swete cloth whil Iuppiter it leste)

I have discussed this line on pp. 42-3. I regard the hexameter as Chaucer's own error.

> 1345. Sk: So greet a routhe I have hit for tendyte
>   Gl: So grete routhe I have hit for to endite   FTBM₁P₁(R₁)
> (G,CAS So gret a reuthe I have for tendite; R₁ *om.* hit)

Hit is very likely intrusive; G,CAS is metrical if one reads *have* as a dissyllable. I should follow G,CAS also in the first part of the line, *So gret a reuthe;* Gl errs in reading *grete* as a dissyllable, for it is obviously of the strong inflexion—*greet.* The G,CAS construction is common (see *L.G.W.* 1045, 1046, 1526, 1632, 1669).

> 1352. Sk: But, as myn autour seith, right thus she seyde   (G),S
>   Gl: .   .   .   . yit thus she seyde   FTBM₁,C
> A,P₁R₁ thus she seyde; PR And *for* But; G *inserts* ȝit *before* as;
> *om.* seith)

It is evident that either *right* or *yit* was in the original text. Of the two I should choose *yit,* for (i) *right* has the authority only of G, which is otherwise corrupt, and of S contradicted by C; (ii) G also reads *yit,* though misplaced; and (iii) inherent and transcriptional probability both favor *yit.* (Note that the contracted forms of *yit* and *right* are easily confused.)

> 1357. Sk: Right so to yow make I my compleyninge   G,CAS
>   Gl: .   .   .   . I make   .   .   .   FTBM₁P₁R₁

The evidence of the MSS. and transcriptional probability both indicate that Gl has taken an erroneous reading.

1362. Sk and Gl: a word on yow, or letter   FTB(M_1)
(G,C(A)S on you a word or lettere; A of *for* on; $M_1P_1R_1$ a *before* letter; P_1R_1 *agrees with* G *in word-order but* R_1 *om.* lese, *and* P_1 *reads* quod she *for* on yow)

I regard the order of words in G,CAS as correct. Either phrase satisfies the metre.

1363. Sk: Al-be-it that I shal be never the better G,(C)(A)(S),(P_1)
    Gl: Albeit I shall be . . . . $FTBM_1R_1$
(CA fayre *for* be; A be hit *for* Al be it; S neuer be *for* be never; P_1 *om.* it)

Though *that* may be an emendation for metre (as it is in P_1) I prefer to take the authority of G,CAS to the single authority of Y_1.

1370. Sk: Of gentil wommen, tender creatures   CAS
    Gl: Of gentil women, gentil creatures $FTBM_1P_1$
(G tendere *in first clause and* gentil *in the second;* R *ends at 1367*)

I reject the Gl reading, because it is founded upon a single authority, and because the repetition of *gentil* is a more likely mistake than the substitution of *tender*. Of the other two readings, that of CAS has the authority of transcriptional probabiliy; for the $FTBY_1$ error would be less natural if *tender* stood in the first clause of *Z*.

1375. Sk: With thyn obeisaunce and thy humble chere   S,P_1
    Gl: With thyne obeysaunce and humble chere G,C(A),$FTBM_1$

The manuscript authority for the Gl reading is overwhelming. Note, too, that the context invites *thy* (the word occurs eight times within six lines). *Obeysaunce* may be quadri-syllabic—so also in 587.

1382. Sk and Gl: that thy sleighte shal be knowe   FB
(T seite *for* sleighte; Th disceyte; C,S set; G,A sekte; M_1 seeyte; P *ends at 1377*)

The $FTBM_1$ reading appears to have been *seite (seeyte);* FB emended this to *sleight* and Th, through a similar idea, to *disceyte*. CAS read *set,* which A emended to *secte*. The latter reading, found also in G, can best account for the variations found in the MSS. The word is used elsewhere in Chaucer in this sense (*C.T.* E 1171).

1386. Sk: wel better love and chere   G,CAS
    Gl: wel better and gretter chere   FTB
(M_1 wel better chere)

The Sk reading is better authenticated. FTBM$_1$ may have had the short M$_1$ line, which FTB emended. *Love* fits both the context and metre—since the final *-e* is elided before *and*.

1406. Sk and Gl: After his fader deeth   FTB
(G,CAS,M$_1$ fadiris—faydrs, fadris)

Ten Brink says (215) that the usual genitive singular form is *fader,* though the form *fadres* is also found. Though the scribes may very well be responsible for the change from one form to the other, the MSS. so strongly favor the *-es (is, s)* ending in this case that I should print it. (All MSS. support *fadres* in 1295, and in 2608 all but C.)

1427. Sk: That ther-in was a ram, that men mighte see (G),CAS,M$_1$
    Gl: That ther a ram was that men myghte see
(G may *for* mighte)

The Gl line is adapted from that of FTB—*That ther was a ram that men myghte see.* With M$_1$ supporting CAS in reading *therin,* there can be little doubt of the reading of *Z;* and since G also reads *therin,* the word undoubtedly was in the original. I cannot understand why Gl should feel that an emendation is called for; *ther-in,* denoting "upon the island," is good enough—cf. *in an ile* (1425), *in the ile* (1463). The metre is correct, for final *-e* of *myghte* may be considered mute (ten Brink, 261). Consequently, I reject the Gl reading as a needless emendation.

1443. Sk: That swich a worship   G,CAS
    Gl: That suche worshippe   FTBM$_1$

Gl would give metrical value to the *-e* of *suche,* a nominative singular of the strong declension. I do not think that the ending can be justified. Moreover, the alternative reading has better manuscript authority.

1457. Sk: Let him go reden Argonauticon   CAS,M$_1$
    Gl: Lét him rede 'Argonauticon'   (G),FTB
(G ryde *for* rede)

Though the reading of this line cannot be determined with certainty, I am inclined to accept the headless line of G,FTB, because the tendency to normalize a line is strong.

1463. Sk: Til in the yle Lemnoun
    Gl: Til in the ile of Lemnon (*All but* A)
(A lond *for* ile)

Sk omits *of* without any manuscript authority. Since the reading of the MSS. is metrical, I see no reason for an emendation.

1471. Sk: Under a banke (*All but* F)
     Gl: Under a brake F
Gl follows F blindly.

1472. Sk and Gl: Where that the ship of Iasoun gan aryve G,CAS
(FTBM₁ Wher lay the shippe that Iason gan arryve)

I accept the Gl and Sk line because it is better authenticated. But I wish to dispute Skeat's statement that the alternative reading is nonsense, for *aryve* may be transitive. (See Chaucer's *Boece,* IV. Met. 3: "Eurus, the wynd, aryved the sayles of Ulixes * * * and his wandrynge shippes by the see, into the ile ther-as Cerces * * * duelleth." See *N.E.D.—arrive,* I. 1—for other quotations.)

1484. Sk: the messagere   CA
     Gl: this messager   G,S,FTBM₁

Sk's authority is practically worthless. He had no excuse for leaving his basal MS.

1519. Sk: And namely, most she spak with Ercules G,C(A)S,T,B,M,
     Gl: And, namely, she spake most . . . F
(A *om.* most)

Gl again takes the single authority of its basal MS. It is obvious that it cannot be defended.

1538. Sk and Gl: As wolde almighty god that I had yive   S
(S *alone reads* almychti; G As wolde god that þat I hadde ȝeue; CA,FTB *om. one* that; M₁ *om. both;* FTBM₁ *reads* y-yive)

I have already stated (p. ⸺) that I regard the readings of G and S as emendations for metre and that Chaucer probably left the line for revision. An editor has his choice of printing either the G or S readings as probably correct emendations, or of accepting the short line. I favor the latter, because I think that neither of the other readings can possibly be Chaucer's.

1545. Sk: Of thise two heer was mad a shrewed lees   C
     Gl: Of these two here was a shrewede les   (*Rest*)

Sk says that the sense and metre require *mad.* But as the passage is punctuated in Gl—a comma after *les* and an exclamation point at the end of the next line—the alternative reading is perfectly clear. It is evident that C emended.

1548. Sk: And Iasoun   G,T,M₁,CAS
      Gl: This Jason   F
(B As *for* And)

This may be slightly preferable to *And,* especially if the line begins another part of the story (as in Gl). But Gl is not justified in choosing a reading when the evidence so strongly favors an alternative which is possible.

1552. Sk: As wolde god I leiser hadde   G,CA(S),(M₁),(Th)
      Gl: As God wolde that I leyser had   FTB
(S,Th *insert* that *before* I; M₁ And *for* As)

Gl has taken the single authority, FTB, contradicted by both M₁ and Th. The Sk reading is clearly right.

1597. Sk: And doth him honour, as hit is to done   FTB
      Gl: . . . . . . as hyt was to done   G,(CAS),M₁
(CAS dyd *for* doth)

Since M₁ contradicts FTB, it is evident that *Z* agreed with G in reading *was.* The past tense makes better sense.

1605. Sk: as real as leoun   S
      Gl: as rial as a lyoun   *Rest*

Sk's authority for omitting the article is practically worthless.

1631. Sk: And of his batail, and in what disioint   G,(CA)S,M₁
      Gl: Of his batayle, and in . . . .   FTB

Either reading is metrically correct: Sk would accent *batail* upon the first syllable; Gl would throw the accent upon the second syllable, and allow for hiatus after the caesural pause —*batayle, ánd* [see ten Brink, 223 (γ),270 (3); also Morris, *The Prologue, The Knightes Tale,* etc. (Clarendon Press Series), p. xlv]. Either reading is logically possible; the omission of *And* gives a different grammatical construction and a somewhat different meaning. Between the two there is not much to choose. I am of the opinion that *And* is not intrusive, for if such were the case, three scribes must have added the word independently. It is more probable that the word was dropped by the FTB scribe. I should accept the Sk reading.

1649. Sk: And gat him greet name as a conquerour
      Gl: And gat a name ryght as a conquerour

Both the Gl and Sk readings are synthetic. G reads *And*

gat hym a name ryth as a conquerour. FTBM₁ om. *ryth* and FB *hym.* C(A)SAd retained *ryth (ryght),* but A changed it to *lyke.* CA reads *gret* for *a;* SAd om. *a* (1). Gl omits *hym* on the sole authority of FB (which also omits *ryght*); FB is certainly wrong, since it is contradicted by T and M₁ as well as by the other two groups. Sk is also wrong in reading *greet,* which has the authority of but CA (CASAd probably read *And gat hym name,* which SAd retains). *Ryght* has the authority of G and CASAd. It appears that G has the original reading, though it is one syllable too long. The line can be read, however, by slurring *hym a—And gát hym a náme—* which is in accordance with Chaucerian usage (ten Brink, 272).

1652. Sk: tresor   G,CASAd
      Gl: tresoures   FTBM₁

The singular form has the weight of authority.

1653. Sk: is she goon   G,CASAd
      Gl: she is goon   FTBM₁

Manuscript authority and the poetical order of words point to the Sk reading as being probably correct.

1657. Sk: And with her lafte his yonge children two   C,S
      Gl: And with hir lefte yonge children two   FTBM₁,A
(G,Ad hire *for* his)

Since G and CASAd (A alone disagreeing) support *his* or *hire,* one of the pronouns was probably in the original reading. Inherent and transcriptional probability favors *his* (it would be very easy to repeat *hire* in this line).

1659. Sk and Gl: And ever in love a cheef traitour he was   FTB,S
(CA thyef *for* cheef; Ad traytour and theffe *for* a thyef traytour *of* CA(S)Ad; A,Ad,G,M₁ As *for* And; G,(M₁) As evere in love a thef & traytour he was—M₁ a *for* &)

The confusion arose through the similarity of "t" and "c."[17] *Cheef* is supported by FTB (contradicted by M₁) and S (contradicted by CA and Ad). The MSS. thus indicate that Z agreed with G in reading *thef.* It appears also that Z omitted *and* (after *thef*); for only Ad—which is otherwise corrupt— has it, though M₁ reads *a* in its stead. Such an omission would account readily for a change of *thef* to *cheef.* Between *And* (FTB,C,S) and *As* (G,M₁,A,Ad) I should choose ⟩*As;* for

[17] Note *coppe* (G,T,f) for *toppe* in 738.

And could easily have been caught from the lines preceding or following. (*As in love*, meaning "in the matter of love," occurs again in 2561.) The best authenticated reading, then, is that of G,(M₁), which is hypermetrical unless slurring is allowed, thus:

As évere in lóve a théf & tráytour he wás.

This is a possible reading (see ten Brink, 272, and lines 55, 56 of the B version of the *Prologue*).

1668. Sk: nas ther noon   G,(CA)SAd
       Gl: nas never noon   FTBM₁
(CA was ther)

Gl has taken a more rugged line upon the sole authority of FTBM₁. I should follow Sk.

1671. Sk: First, whan she of his falsnesse him umbreyde
FTBM₁,Ad,(C),(A)
       Gl: First of his falsnesse whan she hym upbrayde   G,(S)
(S that she *for* she hym; C hym of *for* of his; *om.* hym; A *om.*
his *and* hym)

Z contradicts G as regards the order of words (the apparent agreement of S with G must not be taken too seriously, for S is erratic and is otherwise corrupt in this line). Since the MSS. do not indicate the reading, I should adopt the clearest—that of *Z*.

1682. Sk: And of the laste king   (Ad)
       Gl: Óf the laste kynge   (*Rest*)

Sk's only authority for *And* is Ad, which reads *And specially of*. *And* might easily have been omitted under the influence of *Of* in the preceding line. But with G and *Z*—Ad obviously emended—supporting the headless line, one cannot logically reject it.

1706. Sk and Gl: 'Nay, for hit is no nede.'   FB,A
⟨*Rest* nay sire it⟩

Gl and Sk are clearly wrong. The FB,A agreement is purely accidental, due probably to the similarity of $s(\cdot f)$[18] to *f*. Parallel cases of Chaucer's use of the formal *sire* when a subject is addressing one of noble rank may be found in lines 314 (*sire* omitted by FB), 319, and 505.

---

[18] A makes similar errors in 931—*flyght* for *flyght*—and in 1749—*fteynyd* for *feyned*.

1710. Sk: Go we to-night to Rome, and we shul see   G,M₁,CA
      Gl: Go we to Rome, to nyght, and we shul se   FTB,SAd

The MSS. are badly divided. With SAd opposing CA, and FTB opposing M_1, the Z reading is doubtful. The Sk reading has one point in its favor, viz., the -e of *Rome* regularly elides before the following vowel. In lines 1681, 1691, 1712, 1861, and 1869 *Rome* has a dissyllabic value.[19] In 1776, the only other line in which the word occurs in this legend, the final -e suffers elision before *is*.[20] Such an elision is not allowed for in the Gl reading (but a weak -e may be considered mute when the metre requires it—ten Brink, 261). Consequently, I am inclined to accept the Sk reading as being more in accord with Chaucer's usage and as having the better manuscript authority.

1716. Sk: And prively into the house they goon   C(A)
      Gl: And ful prevely, etc.   (*Rest*)
      (A vn *for* into; S in *for* into)

CA has evidently emended for metre. The alternative reading appears to be an example of dissyllabic anacrusis, which ten Brink says "occurs far less frequently than even suppression of the anacrusis, and should therefore be yet more emphatically repudiated" (p. 216). Ten Brink further asserts that scribes are mainly responsible for both the omission and insertion of superfluous monosyllables at the beginning of the line (pp. 215-6). One might suggest a syncopation of the second e of *prevely;* but such an elipsis, as far as I have been able to ascertain, cannot be defended. Were the MSS. less emphatic in their support of *ful,* one might jump at ten Brink's suggestion that the scribes were responsible for the redundant syllable. But under the circumstances I should accept the dissyllabic anacrusis as representing—as far as we are able to judge—Chaucer's own work.

1717. Sk: Nor at the gate porter was ther noon (*All but* M₁)
      Gl: For at the gate . . . . .   (M₁)
      (M₁ For porter at the gate; CA *om.* the; Ne *for* Nor)

Gl takes the authority of M_1 without a comment. *Nor* is clearly right. Perhaps Gl misprints.

[19] In 1861 S adds *grete.* In all the other cases cited the MSS. are unanimous in their support of the dissyllabic value of *Rome.*

[20] The metrical value of *Rome* in other poems is in accordance with Chaucer's usage as cited here. I have not found a single exception.

1721. Sk: And softe wolle our book seith that she wroghte

(M_1,CA,Ad)

Gl: And softe wolle saith our book . . .   FTB,(S)

(M_1,CA,Ad *om.* that; G *om.* our book; S And thus gate seith our boke; Th And soft woll saith Liui—*probably a marginal gloss*)

Since G is non-committal, one can determine merely the reading of *Z*. The order of words as given in Sk has the better authority, since M_1 contradicts FTB; they also give a smoother line, allowing the accent to fall naturally on *book*. M_1,CA, and Ad are wrong in omitting *that*, however, since *book* (some MSS. *booke, boke*) cannot be dissyllabic. I should print the Sk line.

1727. Sk: so long   G,Th
      Gl: to long   (*Z*)
(A *om.* to)

The true reading cannot be determined. Perhaps *so,* influenced by the preceding *s,* is the easier error.

1728. Sk: For which the dreed doth me so sore smerte   G
      Gl: For which the drede doth me so to smerte   (*Z*)
(A *om.* so; M_1 *om.* to; C drede of deth doth me to smert)

Since the evidence of the MSS. is evenly divided, the reading must be determined apart from such evidence. I should accept *to,* partly because the heaping up of sibilants as in the G line is bad poetry, and partly because *sore* could so easily creep into the line—*sore smerte* is commonly used by Chaucer (see *L.G.W.* 502; *C.T.* A 230, 1394; B 3903; G 871).[21]

1729. Sk and Gl: Right as   FTB
(*Rest* That *for* Right)

That makes better sense, for it correlates with *so* in the preceding line. It also has the support of the MSS.

1736. Sk: And eek her teres (*All but* F)
      Gl: And eke the teeres   F

Gl again follows its basal MS. blindly. *Her* is clearly the better word.

1739. Sk and Gl: For they acordeden in dede and signe   (FTB)
(FTB *insert* in *also before* signe; G,CASAd,M_1 acorde both in; Ad worde and synge; CA worde and Ryme)

[21] In none of these cases do we get *so sore smerte.* Note that Skeat glosses *drede* thirty times, but *dreed* in this line only. (In most cases *drede* is the rime-word.)

G,M₁, and CASAd have a trisyllabic form of the verb *(acorde, acorden, accordyn)* and read *both* before *in*. (Either the trisyllabic or the quadrisyllabic form of the verb is correct; in fact, the latter would probably be read often as a trisyllable.) I should accept the reading of G,M₁,(CA)S(Ad) —*For they acorde bothe in dede & sygne*—a perfectly good line, in preference to an edited FTB line.

1749. Sk: her beautee nas nat feyned   G
      Gl: . . . was not feyned   (*Z*)
(C *om.* not; A steynyd *for* feyned)

See line 5.

1752. Sk: his wit was al forgeten   (G),(CA)SAd,M₁
      Gl: his witte was forgeten   FTB
(G is *for* was; CA all *before* his)

Though *wit* (A. S. *wit*) occurs also in M. E. with a weak final *-e* (*wyte*—ten Brink, 203), I should reject it here upon the authority of the MSS.

1757. Sk: A-morwe   G,CASAd
      Gl: On morwe   FTB
(M₁ And morwe)

A is probably correct.

1764. Sk: Al this conceit his herte hath now y-take   G,M₁,S
      Gl: . . . . . new y-take   FTB,Ad
(C was take; A was I-take)

The change from *now* to *new*, or vice versa, is so easy that the evidence of the MSS. counts for little. The source of the passage (Ovid, *Fasti* ii. 767 ff.) gives no help. Line 1760 —*The ymage of hir recordyng alwey newe*—introducing the three lines in which Tarquinius recalls the beauty and grace of Lucretia's person, and the simile of the water which *wol* * * * *quappe a day or two* after the storm has ceased, suggest that *new* is correct. But one cannot be dogmatic upon such slender evidence.

1773. Sk: 'Hap helpeth hardy man alday,' quod he   G,CS(Ad)
      Gl: . . . . alway . . .   FTBM₁
(A *om.* alday; Ad ffor alday hap helpeth the hardy man)

Alday, in the sense of "continually," "always," is very common in Chaucer. It occurs in two other lines of *L.G.W.*, 1250 and 1877 (so read in every MS.). I should accept it here as the better supported reading.

1782. Sk: Whan every night was to his reste broght
    Gl: Whan every wyght . . . .   G,Z

Sk prints *night* without authority. Apparently it is a misprint. (Note *night* in 1781.)

1791. Sk and Gl: Or if thou   FTB
(G,M₁,CSAd Or if there; A Or if that)

Though *thou* fits the context better, it has the support of but a single authority. The source[22] does not suggest either phrase.

1795. Sk: And sette the point al sharp upon her herte G,M₁,C(ASAd)
    Gl: . . . swerde . . unto . . .   F(T)B
(T,Th on *for* unto; The *for* And; Ad at *for* upon; S,A unto *for* upon)

There can be no doubt that *point* is correct. One cannot determine whether *upon* or *unto* is correct, for a scribal change from one to the other would be easy. *Upon* has the support of the most reliable of the MSS.—G and M—and of transcriptional probability, for *unto* could have been caught from the line preceding.

1801. Sk: Wel wot men that a woman   G,M₁,CA(S)
    Gl: Wel wote men a woman   FTB,Ad
(S wommen *for* a woman)

I should accept the Sk reading, partly because it has better authority, and partly because the dissyllabic form *wote,* if permissible at all, is very unusual; *wot* in the plural should be uninflected and monosyllabic, for it is the result of analogy with the singular form (ten Brink, 198).

1805. Sk: quod he, this cruel man   G,A,SAd
    Gl: quod tho this cruelle man C
(FTB quod this cruelle man; M *lacking*)

Gl has taken *tho* upon a very weak authority. I can see no reason for rejecting *he.*

1815. Sk: She loste bothe atones wit and breeth   CASAd,FTB
    Gl: She lost attones bothe wytte and brethe   (G)
(M *lacking;* G Sche loste bothe at onys bothe wit & breth, *though the first* bothe *has been crossed off with a light line.*)[23]

[22] Utque torum pressit, "Ferrum, Lucretia, mecum est,
    Natus," ait, "regis, Tarquiniusque loquor."

                              Ovid, *Fasti.* ii. 795-6.
[23] Not recorded in the Chaucer Society print.

Bothe (2) in G is more likely to be an error than *bothe* (1). The Sk reading, then, has the authority of all the MSS.

1824. Sk: a vileins dede   CASAd
     Gl: a vilenous dede FTB
(G a vileyn deed; M *lacking*)

The CASAd reading is by far the more common in Chaucer. Skeat glosses *vilenous* only twice—*C.T.* B 2693 and *R.R.* 178. Since the first of these occurs in prose and the other in a translation, I think that it is more probable that CASAd preserves the reading of *Z*. Besides, *vileins* will better explain the G form, *vileyn*.

1825. Sk: But now to purpos   G,C(A)SAd
     Gl: But now to the purpose FTB

In such a phrase *the* is more likely to have been inserted than dropped. And since the evidence of the MSS. and of metre is also in favor of its omission, I should omit it from the text.

1826. Sk: al this mischaunce is falle   FB
     Gl: and this myschaunce is falle T,(CA)SAd,(G)
(CA was *for* is; G befalle *for* is falle; M *lacking*)

Sk has evidently taken an FB emendation.

1835. Sk and Gl: A word for shame ne may she forth out-bringe
                                     FTB
(G,S A word for shame forth ne myght she brynge; C,Ad *agree with* G,S *but read* may *for* myght; A A worde for shame she myght non forth brynge)

Gl and Sk could have avoided the tautology of *forth out* by recognizing the authority of the other MSS. Moreover, *shame* (O. E. *sceamu*) is regularly dissyllabic. I should print the G,S(CAd)(A) line.

1839. Sk: The wo to tellen hit were impossible   F(T)B
     Gl: The wo to telle hyt were an impossible Ad(CAS)
(T,CA,S *om.* hit; G,M *lacking*)

The phrase *an impossible* occurs elsewhere in Chaucer in *C.T.* D 688; F 1009; *T.C.* iii. 525—accented in each case as here. CASAd probably read *The wo to telle[n] were an impossible,* to which Ad added *it.* It is possible that FTB also lacked *hit,* for it is not in T (Th agrees with T). I am of the opinion that CAS(Ad) preserves the reading of *Z*—the only reading we can determine in this case.

77

1846. Sk: That wolde she nat suffre, by no wey   CAS(Ad),(T)
      Gl: That nolde she nat suffren by no wey   (FB)
  (FTB,Ad *om.* nat; G,M *lacking*)

Nolde has the authority of but FB, contradicted by T (and Th). (But see l. 5.) Th also agrees with CAS in reading *nat*, which is required by the metre.

1881. Sk: That so gret feith in al the lond he ne fond   FTB
      Gl: Nat so grete feythe in al that londe he fonde
  (CA Nat; FTBTh *alone reads* the londe; CASAd,M₁ *om.* londe *and read* that *for* the; Ad treuthe *for* feythe; A *om.* ne; G *lacking*)

It will be seen that the Gl line is a hybrid; *Nat* comes from CA, *that* from CASAd,M, *londe* from FTB, and the authority for omitting *ne* from A. Such a line has no place in a critical text. At best it is but an attempt to manufacture a readable line out of the variations found in the MSS.; it cannot explain those variations. M furnishes the clew to the reading of *Z;* for in supporting CASAd it indicates clearly that *the londe* is an FTB reading, caught apparently from the preceding line. *Z* read

       That so grete feythe in al that he ne fonde.

The line passed unchanged to FTBM and CASAd. FTB substituted *the londe* for *that;* Ad misread *feythe* as *treuthe;* CA substituted *Nat* for *That;* and A omitted *ne*. The *Z* line suits the context perfectly and avoids an inartistic repetition of *the londe*.

1883. Sk: And as of men, loketh which tirannye
                         (F)B(TM₁),(CA)(SAd)
      Gl: And as for men, loketh . . . .   (Th)
  (F women *for* men, CA also *for* as; CA(S)Ad,T,²⁴M₁,Th loke ye (S loke) *for* loketh; G *lacking*)

Sk and Gl clearly err in reading *loketh* for *loke ye* (only FB read *loketh*). Though -*eth* is the common ending for the imperative plural, it is "reduced to *e,* or lost altogether when immediately followed by its pronoun."[25] As between *for* (Th) and *of (rest)* one would not hesitate; perhaps Gl misprints.

1888. Sk: Nat for thy sake only wryte I this storie CASAd,(T),(M₁)
      Gl: Nat only for thy sake writen is this story FB
  (T writen is *for* wryte I; M₁ wryte I only *for* only wryte I; G *lacking*)

[24] The Chaucer Society print erroneously reads *þe.*
[25] Emerson, *Middle English Reader* (Macmillan, 1915), cii. See also ten Brink, 189.

Gl follows the single authority FB for the word order and FTB for *writen is* for *wryte I.* The Sk line is clearly the reading of *Z*.

1890. Sk: Of Theseus the grete untrouthe of love   Z(—F)
     Gl: Of . . . . . untrewe . . .   F
(G *lacking*)

Untrouthe, the usual form of the substantive, is undoubtedly correct.

1895. Sk: That hadde an hundred citees   M₁,CASAd
     Gl: That wan an hundred citees   FB
(T þat an C. Citees; G *lacking*)

Hadde was probably the reading of *Z,* because both M and CASAd support it. It is not unlikely that T preserves the FTB reading, which FB emended.

1902. Sk: Alcathoe he bisegeth harde and longe
                          (Th),(M₁),(T),(SAd),(CA)
     Gl: Alcathoë besegeth harde . . . .   (FB)
(M₁ Alcytote, T Alcie, SAd Alcitoe, CA All the Cyte, FB And the Citee *for* Alcathoe; G *lacking*)

Though all of the MSS. stumble over the uncommon name, only FB omits *he.* Gl is plainly wrong.

1927. Sk and Gl: For to be slayn(e), as ye shul after here   FTB
(G,M₁,CA(S)Ad righ as ȝe shal here)

If the evidence of the MSS. counts for anything, there can be no doubt of the correctness of the latter reading. Since the plural form of the P. P. of *sleen* may be dissyllabic— *slayne* < **slayene* < **slaȝene*—the reading of G, etc., is metrical.

1936. Sk: Unto Minos   CA
     Gl: To Mynos   M₁FTB,(S)Ad
(G Theseus—*incorrectly*)

This line has already been discussed (pp. 43, 44). The CA reading can be accepted only as an emendation. (See 1964 below.)

1950. Sk: And in a prison, fetered, cast is he   M₁FTB,C,SAd,(G)
     Gl: . . . . . fetred faste is he   A,Th
(G into *for* in)

Gl is clearly wrong. Though it repudiates its basal MS., it makes no note of the fact.

1956. Sk and Gl: And now, if any woman helpe thee   FTB
(G,M₁,SAd And if now; CA And yef)

Though the agreement of G,M₁,SAd may be accidental, I
should accept their testimony, inasmuch as the meaning of
the line is not affected.

1964. Sk and Gl: Of king Minos, that in hir chambres grete   S
(G Of Theseus; *Rest* Of Mynos)

G errs (see p. 43).   The most regular of the other readings—that of S—is a patent emendation.   I am inclined to
think that Chaucer himself is responsible for either the wrong
name or the rough metre in both this line and 1936.   In each
case I should print the headless line—*To Mynos; Of Mynos.*

1966. Sk: In mochel mirthe   CA
      Gl: Of Athenes   G,FTBM₁,SAd

I have discussed this line on pp. 43-4.   I should accept the
Gl reading as Chaucer's own slip.

1967. Sk: Not I not how   G,T,Ad
      Gl: Wot I not how   FB,S
(M₁ Note; CA But)

Wot appears to be an FB,S error.   But see l. 5.

1971. Sk: His compleyning, as they stode on the wal   G,CASAd
      Gl: His compleynt, as they stoden on the walle   FTBM₁

Both readings are metrical; the extra syllable in *compleynynge* is compensated for by the elision of final *-e* of *stode*
(a common variation of *stoden*) before the following vowel
(ten Brink, 178).   But G,CASAd probably present the true
reading; for it is decidedly easier for a verbal substantive to
lose its ending in one MS. than for the common noun to
acquire the ending in two.

1991. Sk: For if he may this monstre overcome G,M₁,C(S)Ad,T
      Gl: . . . . . the monstre . . .   FB
(S And *for* For; A *ends at* 1985)

The Sk reading is clearly correct.

1999. Sk: That nis nat derk, and hath roum eek and space   SAd
      Gl: . . . . hath roume and eke space
                                             FT(B),(C)
(G hath bothe roum & space; M₁ there ys Rome and space; C,M₁,B
ys *for* nis)

Z evidently read *eek and space* or *and eke space* (M₁ has

80

emended). Of the two, *and eke* is the more natural (Cf. 2021, 2055, 2152, 2153, etc.) and is better supported by the MSS. But *eke* is such a convenient filler that one is tempted to accept the less common G phrase. As regards *ys* or *nis* see l. 5.

2024. Sk: This is my reed, if that he dar hit take   G,FTBM₁,Ad
     Gl: . . . if that ye dar hyt take   (C),S
(C that yef ye)

Both the evidence of the MSS. and the meaning of the passage indicate that the Sk line is correct.

2027. Sk: And whan thise thinges been acorded thus   G
     Gl: Whan these thynges . . .   *Rest*

Whether *And* crept into G or dropped out of *Z* cannot be determined. (See pp. 50-1 for a discussion of normalization of metre in G.)

2048. Sk: To han my lyf, and for to han presence   G,S
     Gl: . . . . and to have the presence Ad
(FTBM₁ and to haue presence; C and also presence)

The authority for the Gl reading is practically worthless; since C, S, and Ad present different readings, it is probable that CSAd was corrupt. Between the reading of G (S has emended) and that of FTBM₁, I should choose that of G, though *for* could easily have been inserted before *to* of the infinitive. The FTBM₁ line is short, for *lyfe* (< O. E. *līf*) is monosyllabic.

2052. Sk: And, him to guerdon, that he shal wel be   G,F
     Gl: And him to-guerdone that . . . .
(M₁,T,B,Ad(C)(S) And him so guerdon)

There is no authority for the hyphen which Gl inserts between *to* and *guerdone* (making *to-guerdon* intensive). Between the G and *Z* readings (for the G,F agreement must be accidental) I should accept that of *Z* as being better suited to the context.

2063. Sk: I prey to Mars to yive me swiche a grace   (G),(SAd)
     Gl: . . . . to yeve me suche grace   FTBM₁,C
(G,SAd so ȝeue *for* to yive; G ȝow *for* me)

The true reading cannot be determined. The article could so easily intrude that I am inclined to accuse G and SAd—which are otherwise corrupt—of carelessly inserting it here.

2075. Sk: And yong, but of a twenty yeer and three   G
     Gl: And yonge, but of twenty yere and three   *Rest*

Sk defends the G reading, considering the article *(a)* as "here used as expressly an approximative result," *i.e., a twenty* means 'about twenty' (Oxford Chaucer, III. 337). With the article missing the line becomes headless (for *yong* cannot be dissyllabic, as Gl makes it). I should accept the headless line, however, for *twenty yeer and three* is a definite number. Somewhat similar phrases in *C.T.* A 2172, C 30, and *R.R.* 1283 lack the article (no other instances are glossed by Skeat).

2079. Sk: Answerde to his profre and to his chere   FTB
     Gl: Answerde hym to his profre and to his chere G,CSAd,(M_1)
(M_1 *omits the second* to)

FTB apparently omitted *hym* for metre. The line should be read

      Answérde hym tó his prófre and tó his chére.

2083. Sk: And leve me never swich a cas befalle   SAd
     Gl: And lene me . . . .   G,FTBM_1
(C let *for* leve)

Sk says that *"lene,* to grant, give, * * * is only used with a following *case;* whilst *leve* is only used with a following clause. *Me* is governed by *befalle."* I do not know what authority Sk has for such a differentiation. The *New English Dictionary* says of *leve,* "With personal *obj.* (? orig. *dat.*) and *inf.* or clause; also *absol.":* of *lene (Lend, v.²),* "with *acc.* and *inf.* or *clause."* (See 2086 below.)

2086. Sk: And leve herafter that I may yow finde   G,(S)Ad,(FB)
     Gl: And lene . . . .   (T,M_1)
(S lyve *for* leve; FTBM_1 *om.* that; C graunt *for* leve)

The MSS. strongly support *leve* here, though in the preceding case they are just as insistent for *lene.* Since the form of *n* and *u* in manuscripts is so often nearly identical, one hesitates to accept the evidence of the MSS. in these two lines.

2092. Sk: Then that I suffred giltles yow to sterve   C,(G,Ad)
     Gl: . . . . . . yow giltles to sterve   S,(FTB)M_1
(G,Ad *om.* to; FTB your gentilesse *for* yow giltles)

M_1 evidently retains the reading of FTBM_1. CSAd probably read *giltles yow,* for both C and Ad contradict the erratic S. Since G agrees with CSAd in this respect, it is more than likely that FTBM_1 erred. Whether we should read *to* with Z or omit it with G (the G,Ad agreement must be regarded as accidental), cannot be determined from the MSS. I think that G is correct, for *gilt(e)les* is usually trisyllabic. Thus in 1982 *And gilteles? now certes,* etc.[26] So in *C.T.* A 1312; B 1062, 1073; F 1318; and *Comp. to L.* 33. In *C.T.* B 643 and *M.B.* 17 it is dissyllabic. Restore the *e* to *gilt(e)les,* and the metre will determine the reading—*gíltelés yow stérve.*[27]

2094. Sk: Hit is not profit, as unto your kinrede   F(TB)
      Gl: Hyt is no profre, as . . .   (G),C(S)Ad,M₁,(T,B)
(G nys *for* is; S to *for* unto; T,B no profit)

F alone reads *not* and FTB *profit.* The MSS. thus support overwhelmingly the Gl reading. (Cf. *Answerde hym to his profre and to his chere,* 2079.)

2095. Sk: But what is that that man nil do for drede (FTBM₁),
                                                  (C)SAd
      Gl: But what is that man wol not do for drede (G)
(G men *for* man; C a man; G nyl *for* wol not; FTBM₁ wol not *for* nil; C wyll do; M at *for second* that)

In spite of minor differences the *Z* MSS. are agreed in repeating *that.* I am of the opinion that SAd retains the reading of *Z;* C misread *nyl* as *wyll* and FTBM₁ expanded it to *wol not.* Since G, reading *nyl* and omitting *that* (2), is short, I am inclined to accept the reading of *Z.*

2134. Sk: Me thinketh no wight oghte her-of us blame   G
      Gl: . . . . . ought us here-of blame (*Rest*)
The true reading cannot be determined. The reading of G is the smoother one.

2138. Sk: And every point performed was in dede
      Gl: . . . . . was performed in dede (*All MSS.*)
(M *lacking*)

Sk says of his emendation, "the improvement is obvious." Elsewhere in Chaucer *performed (parformed)* is either accented on the second syllable or is read as a dissyllable with the accent on the first syllable. Of the lines glossed in Skeat, *C.T.* B 1646; C 151; D 2104; E 1795; and *R.R.* 1178 read *perfórmed; C.T.* E 2052 *párfourn'd:* none read *pérforméd.* So it is not unlikely that Skeat's emendation is justifiable. It is of significance, however, that not one of the scribes made the simple emendation.

[26] FTB,A read *certes now.* Otherwise the MSS. support the reading as quoted.
[27] So Bilderbeck, *op. cit.* 114.

2184. Sk: Allas! for thee my herte hath now pite G
Gl: Allas, for . . . herte hath pitee   FTBM₁,Ad
(C,S hath gret pyte)

Gl reads *herte* as a dissyllable. It is not impossible that G has emended, as C and S have done; for both *now* and *gret* are colorless words.

2215. Sk and Gl: For, thogh so be that ship or boot heer come   C
(*For* ship or boot heer come, G boot here ne cone; M₁ boote here kome; FTB botte noon here come; SAd any bote her come)

I have discussed these variants and Koch's emendation, *never boot here come,* on p. 44n. An editor can do no better, I think, than print the C or SAd reading as an emendation.

2218. Sk and Gl: What shal (Gl shulde) I tell more her compleining
FTB
(G,C(S)Ad,M₁ I more telle *for* I telle more; S of *before* her)

Since M₁ agrees with CSAd and G, I regard the FTB reading as an error.

2221. Sk: But shortly to the ende I telle shal   G,CSAd
Gl: . . . . the ende tel I shalle   FTBM₁

The Sk reading has the better manuscript authority and is better aesthetically.

2229. Sk and Gl: The faire world   FTBM₁
(G,CASAd This fayre world)

I should accept *This* because it fits the context as well as *The* and has better manuscript authority. (See 1991 and 2346.)

2239. Sk: That, whan that I his foule story rede   G,SAd,(M)
Gl: . . . . I this foule . . .   FTB
(C that *for* his; M *inserts* in *before* his)

Since M contradicts FTB and agrees with G and SAd in reading *his,* I regard *this* as an error. The third *that* in C was probably influenced by the preceding ones.

2255. Sk and Gl: This revel, ful of songe and ful of daunce FTBM₁
(G,SAd ek *for second* ful; C om. ek of)

Since it would be easy for a scribe to repeat *ful,* and since two authorities have *ek,* it is probable that *ek* is correct.

2272. Sk and Gl: Unto his fader in lawe, and gan him preye   FB,C
(G,²⁸T,M₁,SAd *om.* and; he *for* him; Ad he gan preye)

I regard *and* as intrusive; the context invites it. The line is metrical without *and,* for *lawe* (A. S. *laȝe, lage*) is a dissyllable. Perhaps the original read *gan he preye* (T,M₁, SAd,G).[28]

2277. Sk: Myself with her wol bothe come and goon   G,C,S
     Gl: . . . . I wil bothe come . . .   FTBM₁,Ad

It is more likely that *I* crept into FTBM₁ and Ad than that it dropped out of G, C, and S. The scribes probably felt the need of another syllable, not recognizing the dissyllabic value of *bothe.*

2286. Sk: To seen her suster, that her longeth so   FTB
     Gl: . . . . . that she loveth so   G,M₁,C(SAd)
(SAd loued *for* loveth)

Since M₁ contradicts FTB, *Z,* as well as G, pretty surely read *loveth.*

2290. Sk: ther was noon her liche (*All MSS.*)
     Gl: ther nas noon hir lyche

Perhaps Gl misprints.

2291. Sk: And yit of bountee was she two so riche   (F)B
     Gl: . . . beaute . . .   G,M₁,T,(SAd)
(F bounde *for* bounte; SAd twyse *for* two)

Sk accepts *bountee* because Chaucer had already extolled her beauty in 2289. I think, however, that Sk is accepting an FB error. The line is plainly parenthetical—though her 'array' was matchless, her 'beauty' was 'two so riche.' Chaucer is translating Ovid's *divitior forma* (*Met.* VI. 452).

2324. Sk: By force hath he, this traitour, doon that dede   G
     Gl: By force hath this traytour done a dede   (*Rest*)

Though G presents the more forceful reading, that of *Z* is probably the original reading; for it is more likely that G felt that the line was short (not giving *force* its full value) than that *Z* should drop *he.* *A dede* is more natural here, I think, than *that dede.*

2337. Sk: And kepte her to his usage and his store   G,C
     Gl: . . . . and to his store   *Rest*

Though one cannot be certain, it is not unlikely that the second *to* is intrusive.

---

[28] In G *gan he preye* is written over an erasure; the original phrase was one or two letters longer.

2346. Sk. this sely Progne   G,M₁,C(S)Ad
       Gl: the sely Proigne   FB
(S *om.* sely)

Gl reads *the* upon the sole authority of FB.

2353. Sk: As hit of women hath be woned yore   G,M₁,C,B,(T *wont*)
       Gl: . . . . . ben y-woved yore S,(F,Ad²⁹ woved)

If the testimony of the MSS. can be accepted, FTBM₁ agreed with G in reading *woned,* which F changed to *woued;* the CSAd reading might have been either. But the letters *u* (for *v*) and *n* resemble each other so closely in the MSS. that the change from *woued* to *woned,* or *vice versa,* is a very simple matter. *Woned* as P. P. is a perfectly good form (ten Brink, 172). But *woved* is extremely doubtful; in O. E., to be sure, the word takes the form of *gewebbod* (Weak II; cf. also the strong verb *wefan,* P. P. *gewefen*); but in M. E. the form is regularly *(y-)woven* (ten Brink, 145, 148). This form—*woven, y-woven*—appears in our text in 2360, vouched for by all the MSS. except T (which reads *woued*). Furthermore, transcriptional probability indicates that *woned* is more likely to be correct. For the scribe has the idea of weaving impressed upon his mind by the passage he is copying; in fact, he has just written the word *weuen* in the preceding line. Consequently, the change of *n* of *woned* to *woued* is a very easy error, or even a perfectly natural emendation. For these reasons I should accept the Sk line.

2354. Sk and Gl: And, shortly for to seyn   F,Ad
(*Rest* sothly *for* shortly)

There is absolutely no excuse for accepting the testimony of F and Ad when the evidence is so overwhelmingly in favor of an equally good reading. (Neither Sk nor Gl notes the variant.)

2356. Sk and Gl: And coude eek rede, and wel y-nogh endyte (FTB)
  (FTB wel y-nogh and endyte; C and also well endyte; G,M₁,CSAd She *for* And; G *om.* eek)

The only authority for *And* is FTB (which is corrupt in another respect); all the other MSS. read *She.* *She* is a perfectly acceptable reading if a period or semicolon be placed at the end of the preceding line; I regard it as correct. But

²⁹ It is not unlikely that Ad also reads *woned;* even with a magnifying glass one cannot tell whether the third letter is a *u* or an *n*.

whether *Z* is right in reading *eek,* or G in omitting it, cannot be determined; I incline to *Z.*

2359. Sk and Gl: So that, by that the yeer was al a-go   S,(C)
(C then *for first* that; G,FTBM₁,Ad *om. second* that)

I believe that CSAd inserted the second *that* as an emendation for metre, and that Ad dropped the second *that* accidentally and C erred in writing *then* for *that* (1). The alternative headless line—*So that by the yere*—is by no means impossible. *N.E.D.*[30] states that *by* was used as a *quasi-conj.* in the sense of "by the time (that)," "by that." The earliest examples cited are the following:

(1297)—R. Glouc., 369.—"By hii aryse * * * Wolues dede hii nymeth
vorth;"
(1444)—Sir Degrev., 961.—"That lady was glad
By sche that charter had rad;"
(1565)—Lindesay—Chron., 31.—(Jam.) "By thir words were said,
his men were so enraged."

The MSS. support strongly a phrase which is in accordance with M. E. usage, but which, apparently, was not nearly so common as the alternative—"by that." Consequently, I think that one is justified in regarding the S and C readings (probably the SCAd reading) as emendations for both metre and clearness of expression.

2360. Sk: in a stamin large   G,CSAd,M₁
    Gl: in a stames large   FTB

Sk says (Oxford Chaucer, III. 343) that *stamin* is correct, being taken from Ovid's *stamina.* The MSS. support his contention.

2378. Sk: her aloon   G,SAd,M₁,T
    Gl: hirself allone   FB,C
Her is correct.

2389. Sk: Doon so as Tereus, to lese his name G,M₁
    Gl: Dóon as Tereus, ...   FTB,(C)(S)(Ad)
(C *inserts* gret *before* name; S *inserts* this *before* Tereus; Ad for lesynge of hys name)

Z evidently did not read *so;* for a word so necessary to the metre would hardly have dropped out of FTB and CSAd independently. The headless line is more likely to be correct.

[30] See *By,* III. 21, d.

2402. Sk: Thus may thise women prayen that hit here G,CSAd
Gl: Thus these wymen prayen that hit here   (F)TBM₁
(F wymen wymmen—*dittography*)

Either reading is metrically and logically possible. The Gl reading is a definite statement of fact—" 'God keep us from such a one!' Thus these women pray." Though such a reading is not impossible, that of Sk is decidedly preferable. Chaucer is just about to tell the story of false Demophon. "A falser lover I never heard of," says he, "unless, perchance, it were his father Theseus. The women who hear this story may well pray, 'God, for his grace, fro swich oon keep us!' " Such an interpretation has the support of the better manuscript authority; I see no reason for rejecting it.

2408. Sk: Ful of his folk   G
Gl: Fúl of folke   (*Rest*)

His strengthens the sense as well as the metre. Though one cannot be sure that G has not emended for metre, I am inclined to accept the G reading.

2410. Sk: And they han at the sege longe y-lain   M₁,(G,SAd)(C)
Gl: And they han at a sege longe y-layne.   FTB
(G,CSAd As *for* And; C *om.* the)

I accept *the* in preference to *a;* for the former has the support of G,M₁, SAd (C omits). But I cannot accept *And* when G,CSAd read *As.* I take *as* here to mean "because," "since"; the line completes the sense of the preceding lines—

(2408) Ful of his folke, of whiche ful many on
(2409) Is wounded sore, and seke, and wo begon,
(2410) As they han at a sege longe y-layne.

Sk, to be sure, gives some point to *And* by making 2410 a complete sentence. But his short sentence is awkward. It is better to accept *As,* which has better manuscript authority and suits the context.

2430. Sk: And to the deeth he almost was y-driven   (G)
Gl: . . . .   he was almoste y-dreven
FTBM₁,(C)S(Ad)
'(G That *for* And; C al to *for* to, ys he *for* he was; Ad ys *for* was)

Transcriptional probability favors the smoother line—that of Sk; for the Z reading—*he was almoste y-dreven*—is that of the scribe's daily conversation. I believe that G is also right in reading *That*—which Sk rejects; for does not the line constitute a clause which completes the sense of the three lines preceding?

2436. Sk: For seek was he
    Gl: For seke he was   *All MSS.*

Sk gives no reason for the emendation; it is entirely un-called for.

2437. Sk: Unnethe mighte he speke or drawe his breeth G,M$_1$,C(S)Ad
    Gl: . . . . . or drawe brethe   F(T)B
(T *om.* he; S and *for* or)

Though *his* may have been inserted by G,M$_1$, and CSAd independently, it is more likely that FTB errs.

2442. Sk and Gl: For at Athenes duk and lord was he   FTB
(G,M$_1$,CSAd For of Athenes)

Since M$_1$ agrees with G and CSAd, *at* is clearly an FTB error. (Cf. *C.T.* A 861. *Of Atthenes he* [Theseus] *was lord and governour.*)

2445. Sk and Gl: in al his regioun   FTB
(G,M$_1$,Ad the regyoun; C,S that regioun)

His is an FTB reading; *the* is correct.

2452. Sk: This honourable Phillis   G,M$_1$,SAd
    Gl: Thys honourable quene   FTB
(C,Th quene Phillus)

The substitution of either word for the other would be perfectly natural. If *quene* were in the original text, the substitution would have had to be made by three scribes independently; a single substitution will explain the readings if *Phillis* were in Chaucer's MS. C evidently added a marginal gloss.

2470. Sk: And wel coude I, yif that me leste so   FTB
    Gl: As wel kouthe I . . . . .   G,M$_1$,SAd
(C I. couthe ryght wel yef that hyt lykyd me)

And is clearly an FTB error, influenced probably by *And* in the preceding line.

2471. Sk: his doing (*All MSS.*)
    Gl: his doynges

There is no adequate reason for rejecting the testimony of the MSS.

2476. Sk: And hath her sworn   G,M$_1$,Ad
    Gl: And to hir swore   FTB,C
(S hath to hir)

Either reading may be correct. But the manuscript authority for the Sk line is more reliable.

2477. Sk: he wolde again retorne   G,M₁,SAd
      Gl: ageyn he wolde retourne   FTB
(C and ageyn retourne)

I accept the Sk reading because it is better supported by the MSS. and because it allows for the elision of the final -*e* of *wolde*.

2496. Sk: 'Thyn hostesse,' quod she, 'O Demophon.' (G),FTBM₁,Ad
      Gl: 'Thyn hostesse,' quod she, 'O thou Demophon.'   C,S
(G Ostesse thyn *for* Thyn hostesse)

Skeat says (in his note on this line) that *hostesse* is trisyllabic. (The word is not glossed in Sk as occurring elsewhere in Chaucer. But cf. *góddessé Natúre, P.F.* 303, 368.)[31] It is more natural to regard *thou* as intrusive than as dropping out of three MSS.

2503. Sk: Or that the mone ones wente aboute   FTB
      Gl: . . . . went ones aboute   G,M₁,C(S)(Ad)
(S ȝede *for* went; Ad yude *for* went, O *for* Or)

The Gl reading is better metrically and has the better authority.

2507. Sk: yif I shal soothly sain   M₁,CS(Ad)
      Gl: yet I shal soothly seyn   FTB
(Ad *om.* yif; G *lacking*)

A very easy mistake would change *yef* to *yet* or *vice versa.* Yet *yif* has the better manuscript authority and fits the context so much better that I should not hesitate to accept it as correct.

2517. Sk: Ther as me thoughte that she wel hath said   (G),M₁,SAd
      Gl: . . . . hath wel sayde   FTB,C
(G *om.* that)

FTB and C unconsciously substituted the word order of daily conversation. *That* is necessary to the metre.

2519. Sk: Ne to thy word ther nis no fey certein   (G,M₁,CAd)S
      Gl: Ne to the worde . . . . .   FTB
(G,M₁,C,Ad is *for* nis)

[31] These two instances are well authenticated. In the first instance only Jo and FB insert *of;* in the second, FB, Lt, Trin, and Cax insert *of* (see Miss Hammond's stemma in the Univ. of Chicago Decennial Publs.). When one considers how strongly *of* is invited in both instances, one must conclude that Chaucer wrote *goddesse* as a trisyllable.

Thy is obviously correct. The MSS. also suggests that *is,* rather than *nis,* should be read. (But see l. 5.)

2523. Sk: Yif that hir vengeance
     Gl: If hire vengeaunce   G,M₁,C(SAd)
(FTB That *for* If; SAd thair—there—*for* hire)

Sk's emendation—*Yif that*—is unnecessary. The line can be read as Gl indicates (giving metrical value to the final *-e* of *vengeaunce*) or as a headless line, considering the *-e* of *vengeaunce* mute (ten Brink, 261). I prefer the latter.

2527. Sk: And on your teres falsly out y-wronge G,SAd
     Gl: . . . falsely out-wronge   FTBM₁
(C *corrupt*)

Though either reading is possible, I should choose that of Sk, because it is more natural and slightly better authenticated.

2534. Sk and Gl: That hit be now the grettest prys of alle FTB
(G That it mot be; CSAd That hyt may be; M₁ That yt moste be; S ʒour *for* the; M pride *for* prys)

Sk and Gl have evidently taken an FTB erroneous reading. I should print the G reading (*mot* has no inflectional ending in the 3rd. sing.), since *mot* accounts for the forms *moste* and *now* better than *may.*

2561. Sk: And trusteth, as in love, no man but me G,M₁,(T),C(S)Ad
     Gl: And, as in love, trusteth no man but me (FB)
(FB truste *for* trusteth; T nowe *for* as—Th *follows* T; S *lacking*)

Gl takes the FB reading except for the spelling of the inflectional ending of the verb. The Sk line is better metrically and is much better authenticated.

2571. Sk: That was of love as fals as ever him liste G,T,(M₁,C)
     Gl: That was in love . . . . .   FB,Ad
(M₁,C *om.* ever; S *lacking*)

Since either reading is possible, I should choose that of Sk because it has better authority.

2583. Sk and Gl: And to this woman hit accordeth weel FTB
(G,M₁,CAd these wemen *for* this woman; S *lacking*)

The agreement of M₁ with G,C(S)Ad leaves no doubt of the correct reading. I regard the G,M₁C(S)Ad reading, with its more inclusive statement—*i.e.,* women in general— as far superior to that chosen by Sk and Gl.[32]

[32] I cannot accept Bilderbeck's statement that *these wemen* refers "apparently to the *Werdys* in 2580." Such an interpretation is quite indefensible. (See Bilderbeck, *op. cit.,* 114.)

2589. Sk and Gl: And rede Mars   FTB
(G,M₁,C,Ad The *for* And; S *lacking*)

I see no reason for rejecting *The*.

2592. Sk: What with Venus and other oppressioun
     Gl: And with Venús, and other oppressyoun   FTBM₁
(G,C,Ad That what *for* And; Th And what; S *lacking*)

Sk's emendation is unnecessary. I should print the G, C(S)Ad line, putting a comma after *That* and reading the second measure as trisyllabic, thus:

> That, what with Venus and other oppressioun
> Of houses, Mars his venym is adoun, etc.

What means "partly"; *what with* is understood before *other oppressioun*. (Gl misses the meaning of the passage by omitting *what*.)

2598. Sk and Gl: That made her for to deyen in prisoun   (G)
(G turne—*caught from 2596*—*for* deyen; M₁ *om.* for to; *rest om.* for)

Though one cannot determine whether *to* or *for to* should be read, one should not overlook the possibility of getting a metrical line by recognizing *made(n)*[33] as dissyllabic. (*Made* is dissyllabic in 1915 and in the B version of the *Prologue*, 162 and 415.)[34]

2602. Sk and Gl: For thilke tyme nas spared no linage   F(T)B
(G,C,Ad was *for* nas; T ne was; M₁ Mars *for* nas; T,C that *for* thilke; S *lacking*)

It looks as if *nas* is an F(T)B reading. (But see l. 5.)

2603. Sk and Gl: to maken mariage   FTB
(G,M₁,C,Ad to make(n) a maryage; S *lacking*)

Though one cannot state definitely that *a* should be read, I should accept the authority of G,M₁, C(S)Ad.

2620. Sk: And thus the day   G,CSAd
     Gl: And thus that day   FTBM₁

I believe that the Sk reading is slightly better than the other. But the agreement of G,CSAd in such a case counts for little.

2631. Sk and Gl: So ny myn herte never thing me com   F
(C *om.* me; *rest* ne *for* me)

[33] Ten Brink states (p. 173, F. N.) that where '*made* occurs as a dissyllable, either *maked* or *maden* should be read'.
[34] In 1915, A gets an extra syllable by inserting the sign of the infinitive, *to;* A adds *to* also in 415; S inserts an *a* in 162. Otherwise the MSS. agree.

Why Sk and Gl should choose *me* for *ne* I cannot understand. Of course it is possible that *me* was changed to the common particle *ne;* but that such was the case is very improbable when only one weak authority reads *me*.

2633. Sk: Tak heed what I thy fader G,M₁,CSAd
     Gl: Take hede what thy fader   FTB

Though *I* could very easily intrude into the line, I should accept it as authentic because of the weight of manuscript evidence in its favor.

2640. Sk: as in this wyse   G,(CAd)S
     Gl: as seyn these wyse FTBM₁
(C,Ad on *for* in)

I believe that *seyn* was caught from *seyde* of the preceding line. *As seyn these wyse* suggests a quoted proverb in the context which does not exist; *as in this wyse* points forward to the 'protestacioun' of line 2642. It is unbelievable that G and CSAd would have changed *seyn* to *in* (*on*) independently.

2649. Sk: lyk as ash to sene   FTB
     Gl: lyke an ashe to sene G,C(S)Ad
(M₁ lyke ash; S like assh on to sene)

I should accept the authority of G,C(S)Ad, especially since the sound of *ash* could easily convert *an* to *as*.

2666. Sk and Gl: And therewith-al a costrel taketh he
                               (G,M₁,CSAd),(FTB)
(G,M₁,CSAd costret *for* costrel; FTB And wyth-al a costrel taketh he tho, *riming with* two *of a four-stressed line*)

I see no reason for printing *costrel* for *costret*. *N.E.D.* gives examples of both forms. *Costret* is the older.

2671. Sk: And go thy wey, lest that him thinke longe   (G),(C),(S)
     Gl: . . . . . . thynke to longe FTB(M₁),Ad
(G,S thynkyth; M₁,C *om.* that; C thynk, Therfore *for* And)

The Sk reading is probably correct, for the insertion of *to* is an easy error. The form of the verb should be *thinke*—subjunctive.

2676. Sk: This Lino and she ben sone broght to bedde   (C)
     Gl: This Lyno and she beth i-broght to bedde
                              FTB(M₁),(Ad),(S),(G)
(C sone byn *for* ben sone; C,S Danao *for* Lino; G,M₁,Ad ben *for* beth; Ad in *for* to; G a *for* to)

Sk prints a modified form of C for metre, though it is obviously a C emendation. One could print *i-broght* for metre (though none of the MSS. has it) or accept the headless line as genuine. I prefer the latter. The form of the verb should evidently be plural—*ben; FTB* alone reads *beth.*

2687. Sk and Gl: She rist her up.   FTB,S
(G,Ad She rist ʒit vp; C,M₁ She ryseth vp)

The reading cannot be determined definitely. In 2680 the MSS. read *She riste hir up* (C *She rose vp*). Perhaps the original reading was *She ryst yet vp,* from which *yet* dropped at Z (the *-yst yet* deceiving the scribe's eye?). In that case the readings of the Z MSS. would have to be considered emendations for metre.

2709. Sk and Gl: And at the window   FTB
(G,M,CSAd And at a window)

Though 2705—*Out at this goter*—suggests that the definite article would be used here, the MSS. strongly support the indefinite *a.*

3. *The "A version" of the Prologue.*

Inasmuch as only one MS. preserves the so-called "A," or revised, version of the *Prologue,* it is obvious that there can be but little opportunity for difference of opinion regarding the text. The Gl and Sk texts differ somewhat, however, chiefly because they follow different principles in mending unmetrical or obscure lines. Note, for instance, lines 127-138, half of which are strangely imperfect in the MS. The MS. presents the lines thus:

(127) Some songyn on the branchis clere
(128) Of loue & that Ioye It was to here
(129) In worschepe & in preysyng of hire make
(130) And of the newe blysful somerys sake
(131) That sungyn blyssede be seynt volentyn
(132) At his day I ches ʒow to be myn
(133) With oute repentynge myn herte swete
(134) And therwithal here bekys gunne mete
(135) The honour & the humble obeysaunce
(136) And after dedyn othere obseruauncys
(137) Ryht on to loue & to natures
(138) So eche of hem to cryaturys

Sk and Gl emend thus:

127. Sk: Somme songen [layes] . . . .

94

```
        Gl: Some songyn on the [      ] braunchis  .  .  .
128. Sk: Of love and [May]  .  .  .
        Gl: [Layes] of love  .  .  .  .
130. Gl: And [for] the  .  .  .
131. Gl: [And] sungyn  .  .  .
132. Sk and Gl: [For] at his day  .  .  .
135. Sk: [They dide honour and] humble  .  .  .
        Gl: [Yeldyng] honour  .  .  .
137. Sk: Right [plesing] un-to  .  .  .  .  nature
        Gl: Ryht [longynge] onto  .  .  .  .  natures
138. Sk: So ech of hem [doth wel] to creature
        Gl: (*Line* 138 *seems hopeless.*)
```

In every case Gl has taken its emendation from a corresponding line in the "B version"; where the line is new, as 138, or so altered that the earlier version gives no clue to the reading, as 127, Gl prints the imperfect line. Sk, on the other hand, makes the text metrical and clear by supplying whatever words appear to fit the context best. The Gl method is obviously the better one.

In several other cases Sk and Gl differ in minor matters of judgment. In 112 Sk mends a headless line by taking *eek* from S; Gl rightly prints the headless line (S is given to normalizing rugged lines). In 34, 189, and 192, Gl emends from the "B" version though Sk does not—(34) *make[th]*, (189) *[hadde] made*, (192) *this [wide] world* (unnecessarily). Sk, on the other hand, emends 232 *(the place)* from the earlier version though Gl does not *(that place)*. These slight differences between the two versions, and others (N. B. 157. *the fret: hir fret;* 173. *the noble quene: this noble quene;* 51. *begynnys: ginneth*), raise the question of whether the scribes were not responsible for many of the minor variations between the two versions. Before accepting these variants as 'revisions,' an editor would do well to ascertain the reason for revision.

4. *General estimate of the Skeat and Globe texts.*

Mr. Pollard says at the conclusion of his brief introduction to the *Legend*, "In making my text I am sorry now that I did not take the Trinity MS. (C) as my starting-point, but I for a long time suspected it of being overmuch edited. Thus the completeness and comparatively good spelling of Fairfax (F) gave it the preference, but in my final revision I have systematically substituted the readings of the Trinity group, or of Gg, for those of the Fairfax where there was any possibility of doubt." The statement is a confession and an apology; evidently Mr. Pollard realized too late that the text he was printing was based upon a very weak authority. Nobody can examine the Globe lines which I have cited in the preceding pages without concluding that Pollard's blind devotion to the Fairfax MS. led him astray constantly. Though many of the Fairfax errors are, to be sure, trivial, many others are such that they obscure the meaning of the passage or lessen its artistic value. Pollard would have gained little, however, by taking C as a starting point, for though C is often right when F is in error, it is at other times strangely erratic (see the long list of C variant readings on pp. 24-5). Pollard made his mistake in not carrying his study of the MSS. further, for he would then have seen that he could put much more confidence in G than he evidently did.

The Skeat text is confessedly eclectic, based upon the Fairfax and Gg MSS.; only in rare instances does Skeat give a reading which is not found in one or both of these MSS. It is interesting to note that Skeat, either because of intuition or because his confidence in Gg proved to be well founded, frequently preserves the true reading when Pollard, in spite of his more thoroughgoing study of the MSS., blunders.[35] Upon the whole the Skeat text of the legends is more nearly correct than that of the Globe; but for the revised (A) version of the *Prologue* the Globe text must be given the preference.

The Skeat text is decidedly preferable as regards textual notes, for Skeat lists most of the variant readings whereas Pollard lists only a few; most of Pollard's notes are Fairfax readings for which he has substituted the readings of other MSS. But there are several important instances in which both Skeat and Pollard fail to give a variant reading, and in some cases the variant proves to be correct (see 1053, 1145, 1382, and 2583).

It must be acknowledged that some of the Skeat and Globe readings which I reject are metrically better than those which the MSS. indicate as correct; in a few cases I reject a metrically normal line for one which is headless; in others I ac-

[35] Curiously enough, there are times when Skeat rejects the reading of Gg and accepts that of Fairfax, while Pollard loses confidence in Fairfax and takes the readings rejected by Skeat. (See 1815 and 2286.)

cept a line which moves awkwardly. But in the vast majority of cases the readings which my stemma indicates as correct are equal, if not superior, to the variants which Skeat and Globe print. Such a result is gratifying to me and compensates for the time and labor I have put upon this work. But even though the results had been otherwise, I should still feel that the work was fully justified; for a true text, no matter how rugged, is of far more importance to students of Chaucer than an artistic though erroneous one.

APPENDIX

1. *Kunz's genealogical tree.*

In the preceding pages I have referred occasionally to Siegfried Kunz's doctoral dissertation entitled *Das Verhältnis der Handschriften von Chaucers Legend of Good Women* (1889). Kunz's conclusions are represented by the following genealogical tree:[1]

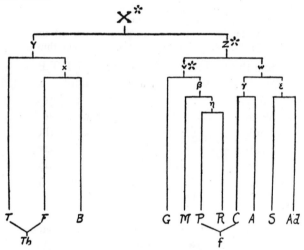

* Indicates MSS. which contained both forms of the Prologue.

Even a slight acquaintance with the MSS. leads one to doubt the accuracy of the table; for it presupposes the existence of both forms of the *Prologue* in at least two transcripts (not counting 'X'), and it can account for the absence of 960-1 from F,T,B,C,A, and S[2] only as due to independent omissions by 'Y' and 'w' or to insertion by 'v'. The chief objection to the supposition that the two forms of the *Prologue* existed in a number of transcripts is the duplication of labor; it is almost inconceivable that a scribe would write two passages of nearly six hundred lines which are very nearly alike. As to the

---

[1] I have altered the designations of the MSS. to correspond with those used in my own work.

[2] This part of the text of Ad has been lost.

absence of 960-1 from six MSS., the mathematical probability is overwhelmingly against the assumption that it dropped out of two MSS. independently and the fact that the details of the story given in these lines are from Chaucer's Latin source (see p. 17) indicates that the couplet was not inserted by 'v'.

A more intimate acquaintance with the MSS. confirms one's suspicions of the inaccuracy of Kunz's table, for many readings cannot be explained upon the basis of the relationship of the MSS. as indicated by the table. The main divisions of his tree rest upon the readings of three lines,[3] in two of which Kunz's judgment is clearly bad and probably so in the third. In the first instance,

1139. F,T,B : For to him yt was reported thus
       G,P,R : But natheles oure autour tellith vs
       C,A : Had gret desyre. And aftyr fell hit thus
         S : And In his hert, than he seid rycht thus,

Kunz rejects the G,P,R reading for that of F,T,B. The readings of C,A and of S are clearly attempts to fill in an imperfect, or entirely blank, line. Both of the other readings are possible. But I think that no one who is familiar with the language of Chaucer would hesitate a moment in choosing the reading of G,P,R in preference to the other. It is a characteristic Chaucerian line (see *Troilus,* I. 394; III. 502, 575, 1196, 1324-5; V. 1037, 1051, 1478, 1563, 1653); I doubt whether the other can be paralleled in any of Chaucer's works.

In the second instance,

1736. F,B : And eke hir (F :the) teeres full of hevytee
    (T heuynesse *for* hevytee; G, M, P, C, A, S, Ad (h) oneste (e)
     for hevytee),

Kunz accepts the F,B reading, thus linking G,M, and P in error with C,A,S, and Ad. But *hevytee* is obviously an error. In the first place, it is an awkward hybrid which cannot be paralleled in Chaucer. In fact, *N. E. D.* notes only one other instance of its use—*Partonope* (*cir.* 1440), line 2466—"The French departid wyth grete heuytee." A second argument in favor of *honestee* comes from the Latin source—"lacrimae. . . pudicae" (Ovid, *Fasti,* ii. 757). Moreover, *honestee* suits the context perfectly.[4] The passage reads:

---

[3] *Op cit.,* p. 16.

[4] The mistake of F,B,(T) probably arose form the fact that the scribe was thinking of the line as a unit and thus lost the meaning of the passage.

And eek her teres, ful of honestee,
Embelisshed her wyfly chastitee;
Her countenaunce is to her herte digne,
For they acordeden in dede and signe.

The third passage reads:

2020. F,B,(T): Than may he fleen a-way out of this stede
Rest: . . . . drede
(T *om.* he)

In this case both readings are possible.[5] The source of the legend does not assist in establishing the correct reading. Consequently, we must fall back upon transcriptional probability. The more natural reading is *out of this stede;* the line and context both invite it. With the phrase once established in a MSS., it is highly improbable that a scribe, in copying it, would substitute *out of this drede.* The principle of 'durior lectio,' therefore, points to *drede* as the original reading.

Kunz presents even a weaker case for the connection of G with M,P, and R.[6] The G,M,P,R reading of *he* for *him* in 1074—

And wel a lord he semede for to be—

is probably correct (though *him* is possible). In 1079 the reading of these four MSS., supported by C,A and partially by S, is undoubtedly correct:

1079. G,M,R,P,C,A: and with that pete loue come in also
(S *om.* in; F,T,B *om.* that *and* in).

Kunz evidntly regarded the G reading as hypermetrical. But the weak *-e* of *loue* may be considered mute (ten Brink, 261). In the third line cited (1003) G,M,P, and R read *schuld(e)* for *wolde* of the other MSS. The difference may easily be attributed to independent errors of scribes (only two scribes are involved). At best it could be used only as confirming stronger evidence, if such were to be found.

The only other evidence which Kunz presents as proof that G,M,P, and R are related is the absence of 960-1 from all MSS. except these four. But obviously the presence of a passage in two or more MSS. can be adduced as evidence of the relationship of these MSS. only if it can be proved that the passage crept into the text in the process of transmission; if the passage

[5] Skeat is wrong in saying (1889 ed., p. 180) that *stede: lede* is an impossible rime-pair. A.S. *stede* comes into M.E. with an open long *e,* and thus has the same quality as both *lede* and *drede.* See ten Brink, 24 (b).

[6] *Op. cit.,* p. 14.

was in 'X', and dropped out of the text during transmission, the close relationship of the MSS. lacking the passage cannot be disputed but the relationship of the other MSS. remains unestablished. Kunz merely assumes that the common possession of the couplet by the four MSS. is proof of their relationship. I am fully convinced that the couplet dropped out of an ancestor of the other MSS. (see my discussion of the point on pp. 16-7).

2. *Bilderbeck's classification of the MSS.*

Though Bilderbeck's work (*Chaucer's Legend of Good Women*, London, 1902), occupies itself mainly with an attempt to prove that MS. G presents an earlier draft of the *Prologue* and the first six legends,[7] it devotes a section (sec. iii) to de-

---

[7] Bilderbeck's arguments to prove that G presents an earlier text of both the *Prologue* and the first six legends are wholly unconvincing. Certain lines of the G text of the *Prologue* are, to be sure, metrically inferior to the corresponding lines of the B version (see A. 127-138); but in spite of these metrical imperfections, the G text of the *Prologue* is undoubtedly the later one, as Mr. J. L. Lowes, arguing from the differences between the two versions and their French sources, has clearly shown (*P. M. L. A.,* 19, 658 ff.). Bilderbeck says, "the differences between the readings of G and of the other authorities in the case of the legends are, in many instances, of the same nature as the differences in the readings of the *Prologues*" (p. 36). But in comparison with the differences between the two texts of the *Prologue,* the differences between the G text of the first six legends and that of the other MSS. are utterly trivial. Bilderbeck points out specifically thirty-one instances (the six legends comprise 1648 lines), mostly changes of single words or short phrases. They include one couplet omitted, 1922-3 (which, as Koch has pointed out—*Eng. Stud.,* 36, 135— could easily have been due to a scribal error, because of the similarity of the end of 1921, *me,* and of 1923, *mo*), and one couplet, 960-1, which Bilderbeck thinks was cancelled by Chaucer but which crept into G,P,R, and M. In a couple of instances Bilderbeck's evidence is weakened because G has the support of other MSS.: 1529. G,CA *no man;* rest, *noon:* 1729. G, CASAd, M, *That;* rest, *Ryght.* Nowhere does the source of a passage help to determine which of the alternative readings is correct—the nearest approach, 1171: G, *sleep,* rest, *dreme;* Ver. *Aen.* IV. 10, *insomnia,* is inconclusive. In three lines G presents a verbal prefix (856. *I-fynde;* 932. *I-offerede;* 944. *I-clepid*) which the other MSS. lack, thus modifying the scansion. Bilderbeck refuses to accept these prefixes as errors of the copyist because "G frequently omits the verbal prefix where many of the other MSS. insert it (see 938: 963: 1637)." If one should comb the text for verbal prefixes, however, one would find that G uses them quite as often as the other MSS. (see 709, 722, 727, 731, 755, 797, etc). The other variants which

scriptions of the MSS. and a study of their relationships. Bilderbeck refuses to draw a genealogical tree because "in the case of some MSS., internal evidence appears to justify a conviction that they are descended from a common ancestor, but is inconclusive in respect to the determination of the number of transcriptions separating the common ancestor from the MSS. compared, [and because] internal evidence sometimes suggests the view that a text is of a composite character [on the same page he mentions specifically P and R as hybrids], betraying obligations of varying extent to different MSS."[8] He summarizes thus: 'G is unique, and the other MSS. may be classified according to their relationships: (i) PR, (ii) CA, (iii) SAd, (iv) M, (v) FTB.[9] The members of Group (i) to some extent take up a position between G and Groups (ii) and (iii). The

---

Bilderbeck cites as proof that G presents an earlier text are as follows (the reading of G stands first): 718. That tho was in that lond Estward dwellynge, That esteward in the world was tho dwellynge; 780. echon, euerychone; 797. And, For; 887. G *om.* noyse; 928. In Naso and Eneydos, In thyne Eneyde and Naso; 944. owne, olde; 1094. Sche, Ful (see p. 103); 1009. at ese was betyr, better at ease; 1112. ffor, To take; to take, to have; 1115. to iuste, the iustyng; 1160. comyth, to; 1168. G. *om.* waketh; *adds* sche; 1170. leue sistyr, dere suster; 1173. me thynkith that, For that me thinketh (thinke); 1175. And ek thereto, And therwith al; 1203. men, folk (folkes); 1212. The hirde of hertis is I-founde, The heerde of hertes founden ys; 1283. Of others landys than of Cartage quien, Of other lande than of Cartage a (S the) quene; 1702. G *inserts* and *before* that; 1727-30. so longe, to longe; so sore smerte, so to smerte; That with a swerd me thynkyth that to myn herte It styngith me whan I thynke on that place, Ryght (S *that*) as a swerde hyt styngeth to myn herte Whan I thenke on the sege (F *these* for *the sege*) or of (S *on*) that place; 1734. And, But [*And* occurs initially in 1732, 3, 5, 6]; hyre eyen let she falle, she let hir eyen falle; 1933. fil, com; 1948. gon, lad; 1984. how so euer, how soothat; 2008-9 as (for *at*) hym lepe, on hym lepe; And slen hym, To slen hym; 2188. G *inserts* al *before* hire. In each case Bilderbeck argues that the reading of G is less desirable esthetically and therefore represents an earlier reading. I should say that almost without exception these variants are the sort of transcriptional errors which are to be found in all the MSS. To be sure, since G is independent of the other MSS., there is always a possibility that G and the other MSS. may present different authentic readings. But the variants which Bilderbeck lists are so different from those of the texts of the *Prologue*—the revised *Prologue* has many new lines, lacks many of the old ones, presents passages in new positions, and introduces changes in words and passages—that one cannot take seriously such minor variations as those given above as evidence of revision.

[8] *Op. cit.* p. 75.

members of Groups (ii) and (iii) seem to be related to one another, and occupy a position intermediate between G and Group (v). Taken as a whole, M occupies a position between Groups (ii) and (iii) on one side and Group (v) on the other. Thynne's edition is for the most part more closely related to Group (v) (to T in particular) than to the other groups."[8] The f fragment he does not classify; he states in another paragraph that it (and PR) "might be neglected, except for the purpose of consultation in the matter of disputed readings."[8]

My genealogical tree (see p. 49) confirms in the main Bilderbeck's summary. But Bilderbeck scarcely does more than arrive at the obvious relationships of the individual MSS.; he does not succeed in discovering the relationship of the several groups. Of what use, for instance, can the fragment f be "for the purpose of consultation in the matter of disputed readings" if one does not know the relation of f to the other MSS.? or the hybrid PR, unless both the nature of the elements entering into the hybrid and the lines affected by each element are known? Moreover, Bilderbeck's qualifying phrases—"to some extent," "seem to be related," "taken as a whole," "for the most part"—and his failure to discover the definite relationships of M (also a hybrid) render his conclusions of little value to an editor.

3. Some corrections of the Chaucer Society prints of the MSS. of the Legend of Good Women.[10]

   1. (P) I *over line by another hand.*
 641. (A) *For* rase *read* rafe.
 837. (M) *For* hydynge *read* bydynge.
 882. (A) ſ *erased before* he.
 890. (G) Myn *written over an erasure by a contemporary hand.* G *apparently read* þyn *or* thy.
1094. (G) Sche manye a beste sche to the shippis sente, sche (2) *being deleted.*
1099. (G) betyr in al hese lyve *in a later hand over an erasure.*
1815. (G) Sche loste bothe at onys bothe wit & breth—*the first* bothe *has been crossed off by a light line.*
1883. (T) *For* lok þe *read* lok ye.
2272. (G) gan he preye *written over an erasure; the original was one or two letters longer.*
2353. (Ad) woued *may be* woned.

[9] I have altered the designations of the MSS. to correspond with those used in my own work.

[10] This list makes no pretensions to completeness. It merely records inaccuracies in readings which figure in my discussion.

INDEX

TO CHAPTER II AND APPENDIX

(Lines discussed in Chapter III are presented seriatim.)